Let me introduce you to my Abba

God and me

—⋈—

Tim Mareglia

Copyright © 2016 by Tim Mareglia

Let me introduce you to my Abba
God and me
by Tim Mareglia

Printed in the United States of America.

ISBN 9781498485838

All rights reserved solely by the author. The author guarantees all contents are original and do not infringe upon the legal rights of any other person or work. No part of this book may be reproduced in any form without the permission of the author. The views expressed in this book are not necessarily those of the publisher.

All scripture is quoted from the "Complete Jewish Bible". Copyright © 1998 by David Stern. Published by: Jewish New Testament Publication, INC., P.O. Box 615, Clarksville, MD 21029.

Word definitions are taken from the "Webster's New World Dictionary of the American Language" Second College Edition. Copyright © 1976.

Hebrew and Greek definitions are taken from "The New Strong's Exhaustive Concordance of the Bible. Copyright © 1990 by James Strong, LL.D., S.T.D., Thomas Nelson Publishers.

www.xulonpress.com

ACKNOWLEDGEMENTS

———∝———

First of all, I want to thank my Abba for His a'ha'va love for me, for the gift of our Savior, Yeshua the Messiah and the salvation He bought for us, for His mercy and forgiveness, for His redemption, for His restoration, for His Hand upon my life and for His constancy. That He NEVER gave up on me and when I returned to Him, He met me with open arms!! Such deep love He has for us, such faithfulness towards us, His children.

I must also thank Him for my wonderful children and their families:

Heather, Joshua, Isabel, Joshua, Madison and Cora

Rebecca, Dan and Eleanor

Let me introduce you to my Abba

Tim, Kelley and Ivy

Emily and Stephen

Anthony, Morgan, Rose, Iris and Roman

Carole Lynn and Mike

Antonina and Dario and

Regina

Children truly are a wondrous "Gift" from our Heavenly Father!!

Alyssa for helping me with the editing.

And a special thanks to my daughter Antonina who helped with the typing.

CONTENTS

Acknowledgements v
Introduction xi

1. Let me tell you about my Abba,,,
   Our Journey Begins 23
2. He knows my Name 33
3. Everything goes back to Gan-Eden
   (the Garden) 38
4. Abba's Words, His Voice 46
5. Abba's Plan, His Way 51
6. The Path We Choose to Walk. 54
7. Returning to a Church Prepared and Our
   Warnings 60
8. Man's Dominion and Decision (We Must
   Choose II) 64
9. Accepting "All" of Life that Comes
   Our Way 67
10. The Father's Constant Heart and Our
    Opportunities to Grow 71

11. We Must Choose III. 75
12. This Body is only Temporary 78
13. Always Follow and Trust Abba,
    It is All for our Good! 82
14. Change is Painful, But it Does Not
    Have to be. 87
15. Let's Revisit the Warnings (II) Again,
    and Some More Change (Pain II) 98
16. The Church Prepared II. 107
17. We Must See Life Through Messiah's Eyes,
    For We are Myopic (Near Sighted)
    We Need His Corrective Lenses 112
18. Abba Does Not Need Our Help, Just Our
    Hearts 114
19. We Must Learn to Recognize the accusers
    Subtleties, For They Are Bondage to Us . . . 119
20. Warnings to the Churches III. 135
21. All of Yahweh's Promises are Ours,
    Including His Punishments 139
22. Our First Love 146
23. Warnings to the Churches IV
    My Chapter 152
24. Covenant. 162
25. It's Truly all about Trusting Abba, It is Our
    Foundation 166

Contents

26. One God, One Messiah, One Holy Spirit and One Church.......................172
27. Birthdays........................... 178
28. Remove These Chains Father and Restore your Church, Take us back to the Garden 181

Introduction

Before we begin I want you to pray a simple prayer of faith, if you have not already done so, to Abba and ask for ***"Wisdom."*** Abba is faithful and will endow you with the wisdom needed to fulfill the call on your life. In this time we live it is so imperative we have wisdom from our Father.

⁵ "Now if any of you lacks wisdom, let him ask God, who gives to all generously and without reproach; and it will be given to him.
⁶ But let him ask in trust, doubting nothing; for the doubter is like a wave in the sea being tossed and driven by the wind.
⁷ Indeed that person should not think that he will receive anything from the Lord,

⁸ because he is double-minded, unstable in all his ways" (James 1:5-8).

Wisdom is that connection between your head and your heart. Your heart (the Holy Spirit) tells you to do something for the Lord, but soon your head begins to talk to you and starts telling you that it was your idea; people will think you are crazy; it won't happen; etc... Once wisdom kicks in, you take those thoughts captive and replace them with God's Word. Now your head is subject to your heart and you are in proper order and able to walk out that Divine appointment.

I believe Abba asked me to write this tome; it is a small part of His bigger story. None of us have the entire story or all of the answers, so I share with you my part. It is meant to encourage you, to bolster and to prayerfully grow your faith, trust, and understanding of the God of Abraham, Isaac and Jacob: our God, our Abba!

It started over three years ago in August, in the middle of my divorce, when I returned to Him after years as the prodigal son. Abba still loved me, still spoke to me, still taught me, and still had His hand upon my life! Just as in the bible, Abba welcomed

Introduction

me home with open arms and held a banquet in **"My honor."** **Wow!!** Such love I have never felt; it was as though I were never gone. No dunce cap, no go stand in the corner, just true, deep, a'ha'va love, unconditional love, love without expectation. Actually, He just reminded me, it started in 1995 when He asked me to start reading the bible from Genesis and to throw away **everything** I had learned through the years. I should add that this was a painful process, for change is painful.

Please understand, I am not an author and never would I have had the thought to write a book. It was only after a year or so of God asking and me dragging my feet and making every excuse I could think of that I relented. For me, it was an issue of trust. I loved Him, but never truly, completely trusted Abba. Trust is something we learn. He reminded me that He would make the words flow, and He did. Most of this was written between 0400 and 0600. He would wake me and I knew I had to write, so I did. I literally read many of my notes and have no recollection of ever having written them, but it is my handwriting.

He began pouring into me His love, showing me through His Word who He really is. The Word came alive to me like never before and it began to make so much more sense.

[12] *"See, the Word of God is alive! It is at work and is sharper than **ANY** double-edged sword- it cuts right through to where soul meets spirit and joints meet marrow, and it is quick to judge the inner reflections and attitudes of the heart"* (Hebrews 4:12).

I began to trust His every Word more than in the past, to read without prejudice, letting Abba pour into me. My trust in Him, in His Word began to grow then, but would take a detour for a while. Do understand, this was about six years before my prodigal years, my detour.

As I began to read, Abba began to speak to me about different things we do in the church that you find no reference for in the bible and one thing we celebrate that is in the bible, but nowhere do you find it being a positive event, a good thing; in fact, its origin is pagan. Some of these things I will cover as you read on. He also led me to a book written in 1853, by Alexander Hislop, called, "The Two Babylon's." The author takes you, basically, from just after the flood, at the time of Nimrod, and gives

Introduction

you a detailed account of the history of paganism. His premise for writing the book I will not comment on, for only God knows that truth.

My hope and prayer is that this book will help you understand **Abba's plan** for you. How your life has made you who you are today. **EVERYTHING**, good or bad, that has happened to you has brought you to **this point**. All the events of your life brought you into your relationship with Abba today. For it was your life to this point that molded you into who you are. I must add there were many decisions and choices that were made during your life that were a part of this process. Some of those decisions and choices were good and some not so good. Does this sound familiar to you? Sometimes we are not the best decision makers; sometimes we are goats instead of sheep, we run amok rather than follow the Good Shepherd.

I am no different than anyone else, so let me make this personal. Anywhere along the way I could have turned my back on God completely, but I could never do that. In all my anger towards Abba, I still knew He was real, He is who He said He is and that He loved me. I just did not understand why He did not take my pain away, why something's happened to me when

He was protecting me. He said He loved me... I used to ask Him to love me a little less. It took me many years to realize He was always there, always loving me. I just did not recognize His presence in my life. The intent also is to stop apologizing for who God is. Abba requires no apologies for Himself, for His actions, for His Word or for His heart. It is truly meant to be a quick read, one day or one sitting possibly: Reread and digested. All scriptures are past, present and future, for it is all about God and all for our edification. Another important factor is how we treat each other. I do not believe God is pleased with the racism, bigotry and/or anti-Semitism He sees in His Church today.

In Zechariah 8:14-17, Abba is giving instructions to the people on proper behavior one to another. Also read Isaiah 58.

[14] "For Adonai-Tzva'ot (Lord of Sabaoth, Lord of Heaven's armies, Lord of Hosts) says, 'Just as I resolved to do you harm when your forefathers provoked me,' Adonai-Tzva'ot says, 'and I did not relent;

[15] so now, I resolve to do good to Yerushalayim (Jerusalem) and to the house of Y'hudah (Judah). Don't be afraid!

Introduction

¹⁶ These are the things you are to do: speak the truth to each other; in your courts administer justice that is true and conducive to peace;

¹⁷ don't plot harm against each other; and don't love perjury; for all these things I hate', says Adonai."

I believe the context of Micah 6:8 is very appropriate here also: *⁸ "Human being, you have already been told what is good, what Adonai demands of you-no more than to act justly, love grace, and walk in purity with your God."*

You will find redundancy as this is written. When you read this, there will be sections that are similar to others, but the intent is as a reminder from a slightly different perspective. When compiling my notes, I had much concern over this, but God reminded me of the redundancy of His Word. This gave me a lot of comfort in realizing I am not alone, and I have wonderful company in this urgent repeating.

I need to be reminded often of His love, grace, and concern over me. That He is in **CONTROL** and the reality is it is my desire to leave my Abba at the helm. He knows every event, every atom of His creation. Why would I ever concern myself over anything, except to pray, ***"Thy will be done on earth as***

it is in Heaven." For if I am ever in His will, I am in a place where He wants me, where He has placed me. **I am in His perfection!**

The one thing you must know with **1000% surety;** is that Abba loves you with a constant love that is unconditional, nor is it temporary. His love for you does not waiver or change. Abba's love is deeper than our comprehension. Our love for Him is only as deep as is our trust in Him, believing in and trusting in who He says He is. I hope and pray you understand and take deep inside you this truth.

[1] "At that moment the talmidim (disciples) came to Yeshua (Jesus) and asked, 'Who is the greatest in the Kingdom of Heaven?'
[2] He called a child to Him, stood him among them,
[3] and said, ***'Yes! I tell you that unless you change and become like little children, you won't even enter the Kingdom of Heaven!***
[4] So the greatest in the Kingdom is whoever makes himself as humble as this child.
[5] Whoever welcomes one such child in my name welcomes me;
*[6] and whoever ensnares one of these **little ones who TRUST ME**, it would be better for him to have*

a millstone hung around his neck and be drowned in the open sea!'" (Matthew 18:1-6).

¹³ "People were bringing children to Him so that he might touch them, but the talmidim rebuked those people.

¹⁴ However, when Yeshua saw it, He became indignant and said to them, 'Let the children come to me, don't stop them; for the Kingdom of God belongs to such as these.

*¹⁵ **Yes! I tell you, whoever does not receive the Kingdom of God like a child will not enter it!**'"* (Mark 10:13-15).

Yeshua is talking to the people and He tells them they must be like the little children who **trust Him** to enter the kingdom of God. Anyone who has children knows they have complete trust in you as a parent, as an adult. They are dependent upon you for **EVERYTHING:** food, shelter, safety, love,,, all of their needs. If you say the moon is made of cheese, they believe you, for they **trust** you **completely**. Why shouldn't they? You love them, you would never deceive or hurt them. Abba desires childlike trust, complete and unwavering, not doubting, not situational, **ever trusting!!**

> ⁵ "**TRUST** in Adonai with all your heart; do not rely on your own understanding.
> ⁶ In all your ways acknowledge Him; then He will level your paths" (Proverbs 3:5-6).
> ⁴ "Look at the proud: he is inwardly not upright; but the righteous will attain life through **TRUSTING** faithfulness" (Habakkuk 2:4).
> ³ "For loving God means obeying His commands. Moreover, His commands are not burdensome,
> ⁴ because everything which has God as its Father overcomes the world. And this is what victoriously overcomes the world: our **TRUST**" (1 John 5:3-4).

But one of the most telling scriptures about trust comes from our Messiah Yeshua, from His mouth to our ears:

> ²⁸ "So they said to Him, 'What should we do in order to perform the works of God?'
> ²⁹ Yeshua answered, 'Here's what the work of God is: to **TRUST** in the one He sent!'" (John 6:28-29).

We must have a strong proper foundation to build our life upon in God and I believe the cornerstone of that foundation is faith and trust in Abba. We must believe that He is who He says He is, that He did what He said He did, and will accomplish what He said He would!

^{24} *"So everyone who **hears these Words of mine and acts on them** will be like a sensible man who built his house on bedrock.*
^{25} *The rain fell, the rivers flooded, the winds blew and beat against that house, but it didn't collapse, because its foundation was on rock.*
^{26} *But everyone who hears these Words of mine and does not act on them will be like a stupid man who built his house on sand.*
^{27} *The rain fell, the rivers flooded, the wind blew and beat against that house, and it collapsed- and its collapse was horrendous!"* (Matthew 7:24-27).

In order to act upon *"these Words of mine,"* one must have faith and trust in the Author, that His words are true and accurate. We must build our faith and trust through the Word.

*^{17} "So **trust** comes from what is **heard**, and what is heard through a **Word** proclaimed about Messiah"* (Romans 10:17).

Truly, I do not believe Abba could make it any clearer to us, **trusting** Abba is the key to our life in Him. Without trust we have nothing but ourselves, which really equates to less than nothing!!
Text from the bible is taken from the, "Complete Jewish Bible," Translation by David Stern.
Abba, may our faith and trust be built upon You, our Rock, and may all the words contained here be about You and Your love for us, and Your relationship with us, Your children. Open our eyes, unstop our ears, and soften our hearts to hear, see, and take your Word, Father, into our hearts. May Your words become our life.

Chapter 1

Let me tell you about my Abba... Our Journey Begins

To tell my story I must begin at... the beginning. He has always been, has always existed, He was there from....forever. This I do not question, though I do marvel at the thought. This is not a thought which causes me any conflict or doubt. If anything, it causes me to trust and believe in Him more. You may question why? The answer is very simple: I live on the earth that He said He created. I can see, hear, smell, taste and touch it. I can experience it with the senses Abba gave me at creation. I experience it every moment of every day. I am in awe of how intricately woven His universe is and how everything in it is so closely knit together. The

more I learn, the deeper my trust and faith is in Him. Scientists ask you to trust their theories, but they are just that, theories. It is truly a matter of trust and as for me; **I prefer to trust my Abba!**
God spoke the universe into existence. He set everything we see and can't see into motion. The entire splendor we see, everything we touch has His signature on it. Nothing was created that was not needed, everything has a purpose, a need, a function. Everything has the fingerprints of God on it! There is a balance of nature that was thought out. Therefore, there is **never a surprise with God, never a time where He had no understanding of what He had done, what He had created, and He is in control of His creation!**

[18] *"What is revealed is God's anger from heaven against all the godlessness and wickedness of people who in their wickedness keep suppressing the truth;*
[19] *because what is known about God is plain to them, since God has made it plain to them.*
[20] *For ever since the creation of the universe His invisible qualities- both His eternal power and His divine nature- have been clearly seen, because*

they can be understood from what He has made. Therefore, they have no excuse" (Romans 1:18-20).

True science, on an almost daily basis, proves His existence by confirming what He has already told us in His Word, a Word which was written long before man's ability to scientifically delve into the fine details and intricacies of our universe. God does not require we prove His existence; all we need to do is introduce Him to a hurt and dying world. The beginning of man's discoveries were based upon something which he knew, something he could see, that which he could touch and/or measure. He started with something and that something is something which God created. This is a simple truth, it is not meant to be profound, philosophical or deep, just trusting and true.

The field of science, the study of our universe did not start in a vacuum, but with that which was already here. The explanation for all we see is spelled out in God's Word. Abba spoke all into existence, except man, whom He formed from the earth and then with His breath breathed life into him, into each of us.

*⁷ "Then Adonai, God, formed a person [Hebrew: Adam] from the dust of the ground [Hebrew: Adamah] and **breathed into his nostrils the breath of life, so that he became a living being**"* (Genesis 2:7). *⁵ "Thus says God, Adonai who created the heavens and spread them out, who stretched out the earth and all that grows from it, **who gives breath to the people on it** and spirit to those who walk on it"* (Isaiah 42:5). Wow! Our breath is a gift from our Abba.

In God's spoken Word were contained all the physical characteristics, all the laws of physics, the attributes and qualities of **EVERYTHING!!!** Stop and ponder that for a day. **Literally in His Word were contained all**, not some, but **all, everything. His Words for us and over us are as powerful!** Let me expound on this.

There are no shazams with my Abba; He does not sit on his throne talking with His Son, or His heavenly host and marvel at man's discoveries about His creation: that the moon affects Earth's gravitational pull, that it affects the tides around His world. That law was contained in *His Word*, all the laws governing the physical characteristics of all types of light were contained in, *"light be, light was."* The specific ph range in our blood: the O_2 content of our atmosphere, the atomic weights of the earth's elements, Avogadro's number. **Everything, not some things, but everything was thought through to the smallest of details!**

When scientists make their discoveries, they are uncovering or discovering our Abba's plan, Abba's Word. They are discovering what He created, the laws He set into motion with His Word! I will say it again: there is **NOTHING** that happens or is discovered where He says, "I am so surprised, I did not know that." I must say this again: there is **NOT THE SMALLEST OF DETAILS** that is a surprise! Please understand and let this picture sink deep into your heart. The inner workings for all we see, hear, smell, taste and touch, and some we cannot, were set in motion by God in His Word. Life for every species, for all the laws of physics that govern inanimate objects, rocks, water, gases, everything that governs their attributes and characteristics were contained in His Word. It is all His design, His creation, His doing. It was **all in His Word.**

When we see and comprehend the intricacies of this earth, this universe, then understand that Abba has prepared something grander for us. We are getting a glimpse of His heart, the heart of the Father, Our Abba:

[9] *"But as the Tanakh says, 'No eye has seen, no ear has heard and no one's heart has imagined all the things that God had prepared for those who love Him'"* (1 Corinthians 2:9).

I truly cannot state this enough, for it is the basis for everything we believe. Without the belief and **trust** in His Word (in Him), we have nothing. If you cannot trust His Word you have no foundation for anything else. Genesis does not start out with, "I have a fairy tale I want to tell you," Abba **s**tarts out with

[1] *"In the beginning **God created** the heavens and earth"* (Genesis 1:1).

Science is no different in that if you cannot trust that one plus one equals two, all else is for naught. All of science is math, and our Abba is **THE MATHEMATICIAN**!! God set up His mathematical universe we live in. Think about it: **math is involved**

in every single entity in this universe, in every single thing. There is nothing in which math is not involved.

[1] *"In the beginning was the Word and the Word was with God and the **Word was God**"* (John 1:1).

Don't you just love how God is so consistent in His Word? Genesis 1:1 and John 1:1 both start out with, "In the beginning." Genesis goes on to tell us of what God did with His Word and John tells us he is His Word.

He is His Word, Messiah Yeshua is the Word! In both the Old and New Covenants, God is very clear about how man should not add to or take away from His Word. He is very zealous and jealous over His Word, after all, it is Him!

[2] *"In order to obey the mitzvot (laws) of Adonai your God which I am giving you, **do not add to what I am saying, and do not subtract from it**"* (Deuteronomy 4:2).

[1] *"Everything I am commanding you, you are to take care to do. **Do not add to it or subtract from it**"* (Deuteronomy 13:1).

⁵ *"Every Word of God is pure; He shields those taking refuge in Him,*
⁶ ***Don't add anything to his Words; or He will rebuke you, and you, found a liar***" (Proverbs 30:5-6).

¹⁸ *"I warn everyone hearing the **words** of the prophecy in this book that **if anyone adds to them, God will add to him the plagues written in this book.***

¹⁹ ***And if anyone takes anything away from the words in the book of this prophecy, God will take away his share in the Tree of Life and the holy city, as described in this book***" (Revelations 22:18-19).

All of these scriptures give an account of Abba's care and concern over His Word, but Numbers 23:19 and Isaiah 55:11 tells us of the truth, power and strength of His Word:

¹⁹ *"God is not a human being who lies or a mortal who changes his mind. **WHEN HE SAYS SOMETHING, HE WILL DO IT; WHEN HE MAKES A PROMISE, HE WILL FULFILL IT***" (Numbers 23:19).

¹¹ *"So will My Word be which goes forth from my mouth; **IT WILL NOT RETURN TO ME EMPTY, WITHOUT ACCOMPLISHING WHAT I DESIRE, AND WITHOUT SUCCEEDING IN THE MATTER FOR WHICH I SENT IT"*** (Isaiah 55:11).

By giving us the Bible and telling us it is Him, God is giving us a glimpse of the awesome power of Himself through His Word. Once again, it is Him! He speaks about His character, His love, His plan, His faithfulness towards us as His children throughout His Word. Are you seeing this picture? Do you see His power and love in this? Are you beginning to see how you may trust Abba, **trust His love without question?** How His Word is **POWERFUL!!!** It is complete and it does not require our seal of approval, our telling Him what it means. Please understand, God, who created this universe, has not lied or been deceptive to us in His Word! And He certainly did not require an editor to make sure what He said was correct and true! Nor that there were a few chapters requiring more words to fill in the column, page, or chapter. **IT IS COMPLETE!!!**

In John 14:2, Yeshua is telling us He does not lie or deceive:

*¹⁴ "In my Father's house are many places to live. **If there weren't, I would have told you**; because I am going there to prepare a place for you."*

And in 2 Timothy 3:16-17:

*¹⁶ "All scripture is God-breathed and is valuable for teaching the **truth,** convicting of sin, correcting faults and training in right living;*
¹⁷ thus anyone who belongs to God may be fully equipped for every good work."

Abba talks to us all through His creation, His Universe, and through His written Word. Every time **ANYONE** reads His Word they are hearing His Voice. Sometimes He will have a very special message for us, and other times He just wants to talk to us to strengthen and encourage us in our daily walk. To be our loving Father, to be our Abba.

Oh Abba, speak Your Words of life over us. Unstop our ears, open our eyes, and soften our hearts as we daily seek you and strive to do your will, as we allow you to live your life through us.

Chapter 2

He knows my Name

———∝———

He knew me, my name, my life, even before I ever existed on earth. For He had a plan for me, for you, for us:

[11] "*For I know what plans I have in mind for you, says Adonai, plans for well- being, not for bad things; so that you can have hope and a future*" (Jeremiah 29:11).

[24] "*Here is what Adonai says, your Redeemer, He who formed you in the womb...*" (Isaiah 44:24).

[13] "*For You fashioned my inmost being, **You knit me together in my mother's womb**.*

[14] *I thank You because I am awesomely made, wonderfully; Your works are wonders- I know this very well.*

15 My bones were not hidden from You when I was being made in secret, intricately woven in the depths of the earth.

16 Your eyes could see me as an embryo, but in Your book all my days were already written; my days had been shaped before any of them existed" (Psalms 139:13-16).

23 "Examine me, God, and know my heart; test me, and know my thoughts.

24 See if there is in me any hurtful way, and lead me along the eternal way" (Psalms 139:23-24).

Abba created us and knew us from the foundation of time. He knows, reads, and judges our hearts through our actions. Up until Messiah Yeshua came the law was about **"physical actions."** When Yeshua came He made it about our hearts, about what comes out of them. It was no longer about physically doing something, but an issue of our heart; it became a thought issue. You no longer had to **"physically do"** something to be in sin, all one must now do is to think it. Abba wants your heart, He wants that we should follow Him in all things. Our thoughts unchecked lead to the physical act of sin. It is all about our hearts!

¹³ *"No one being tempted should say, 'I am being tempted by God.' For God cannot be tempted by evil, and God himself tempts no one.*

¹⁴ *Rather each person is being tempted whenever he is being dragged off and enticed by the bait of his own desire.*

¹⁵ *Then, having conceived, the desire gives birth to sin; and when sin is fully grown, it gives birth to death"* (James 1:13-15).

We read in 1 Samuel 13:14

¹⁴ *"But as it is, your kingship will not be established. Adonai has sought for Himself **a man after His own heart**, and Adonai has appointed him to be prince over His people, because you did not observe what Adonai ordered you to do."*

Also, in Acts 13:22:

²² *"God removed him and raised up David as king for them, making His approval known with these words, **'I found David** Ben-Yishai to be a **man after my own heart; he will do everything I want.'"***

We have Saul being removed as the King over Israel because he did not obey God's Word and *"King David a man after God's own heart,"* being anointed as the new King because he would do what God wanted him to do. David would be obedient to Abba's Word and not men! David fully trusted his God! Abba was confident! For He knew David's heart.

King David did not always do what was right, for he was a flawed man, but David also understood that Yahweh was a just God and would punish the wicked. He also knew that Abba was always faithful and willing to forgive the truly repentant heart when confronted with his sin. David's heart was always towards God, for King David had a profound understanding that all of life was about God and not about himself, that God would, in fact, punish the unrepentant person. David understood it was about relationship and trust. The theme of David's writings is much about trusting and praising Abba.

In keeping with the heart, I believe two of the reasons why God created us were for fellowship, which includes our praise and worship of Him, and the second being His love of our creativity in Him. God truly loves our creativity in Him. Our Abba loves praise; I believe the command to praise Him is possibly one of the most often written **commands** for us in His Word. Think how often the word praise is used in Psalms alone.

I believe praising our God should be one of our most joyful responsibilities of fellowship we can have with and for our Father. He loves His creation and His desire is to have close fellowship with His creation. (I will often use creation versus just saying man, for God loves His animals, trees, sky...all that He created).

Abba may our prayers and praises be a fragrant offering to you. Abba, restore your worshippers in your Body, come inhabit our praises to you. Abba, may we experience life through your perfection and not through our flawed perspective.

Chapter 3

Everything goes back to Gan-Eden (the Garden)

———⋈———

God created man and placed him in Gan-Eden (The Garden of Eden). There God walked and talked with him, He saw that man was alone, so He created woman so man would not be alone. Then Abba himself walked in the cool of the evening with Adam and Eve. Personally, I love how God, in the lower animal world, made the male the beautiful specie, but in humans, guys face it, the female is more beautiful than the male.

At some point in time in God's heavenly realm there was an insurrection by God's right hand angel who wanted to take God's place as The Most High. Truly, there is very little written about the accuser's rebellion, but he is mentioned many times in God's Word. The accuser and his followers, his angels, rebelled and were subsequently thrown out of His kingdom where they became an army, and the battle for Abba's kingdom began in earnest. At this time, he and his followers were given new names. Lucifer became the accuser and his angels became demons. A "physical" battle began for the kingdom.

Yeshua in Matthew 11:12 talking to His disciples tells them:

[12] *"From the time of Yochanan the Immerser* (John the Baptist) *until now,* **the Kingdom of Heaven has been suffering violence; yes violent ones are trying to snatch it away."**

I am retired military and understand very well the concept of force, of war. It is not a two out of three chess match, a best of seven "World Series", but a physical, violent battle illustrated very well in Frank Peretti's books. Mr. Perretti, I believe, captures this battle very accurately in his stories; it is a violent physical battle.

So in Exodus 14:13-14 Moshe (Moses) speaks to the Hebrew children because of their complaining and fear:

¹³ "Moshe answered the people, 'Stop being so fearful! Remain steady, and you will see how Adonai is going to save you. He will do it today-today you have seen the Egyptians, but you will never see them again!
*¹⁴ "**Adonai will do battle for you**. Just calm yourselves down!'"*
*¹⁵ "He said, 'Listen, all Y'hudah (Judah), you who live in Yerushalayim (Jerusalem) and King Y'hoshafat (Jehoshaphat): here is what Adonai is saying to you: 'Don't be afraid or distressed by this great horde; **for the battle is not yours, but God's**'"* (2 Chronicles 20:15).
*⁴⁷ "and everyone assembled here will know that Adonai does not save by sword or spear. **For this is Adonai's battle, and He will hand you over to us**"* (1 Samuel 17:47).
¹² "For we are not struggling against human beings, but against the rulers, authorities and cosmic powers governing this darkness, against spiritual forces of evil in the heavenly realm" (Ephesians 6:12).

Therefore, when Abba says, *"This battle is not yours, but Mine,"* this battle, this war, began between God and the accuser. It did not begin with us, though we are now pawns in this war. We were at this time just a thought of God's, a plan. This battle is truly His, He fights for us. God knows and understands we are not capable on our own to do battle with satan and his minions, so he battles for us. We stand in His strength; it is Him, not us. His expectation for us in the battle is to trust and believe in Him, to resist the accuser and just stand firm in our Savior who did in fact defeat satan at the cross. It is up to us to resist and stand in and on that promise, for **"the battle truly belongs to the Lord."** This is God's Word for us:

[7]**"Therefore, submit to God. Moreover, take a stand against the adversary, and he will flee from you"** (James 4:7).

A war is comprised of thousands of battles and skirmishes, but in the end the war is won by the last man standing. If you were to speak with the men and women heading into battle, they would tell you there is a detailed battle plan and they could tell you of the anticipated outcome. But, they also know and would tell you there are no guarantees. In the war with the accuser, in this violent battle, there are people who are lost, those people whose trust and faith and roots are shallow. This though is not a measure of God's success. We know this because of Yahweh's Word. Through His Word we know the outcome, we can have **1000% confidence in that outcome**. Yeshua defeats the accuser once and for all and sends him to hell. Defeat is not the right word. Yeshua defeated the accuser at Calvary, but in the final battle, Messiah will remove satan from any form of dominion over His people for the 1000 year reign!

We can look to the Hebrew children's desert experience to see how in every battle God went before and promised victory because of Him, not because of them, but for them. A couple of times they struck out on their own and were defeated, soundly defeated! This is a warning for us. We cannot go out on our own, we must have Abba as our leader, as our Commander in Chief and we follow Him. He does not follow us.

[41] *"Then you answered me, 'We have sinned against Adonai. Now we will go up and fight, in*

accordance with everything Adonai our God ordered us.' And every man among you put on his arms, considering it an easy matter to go up into the Hill-country. ⁴² But Adonai said to me, 'Tell them, don't go up, and don't fight, because I am not there with you; if you do, your enemies will defeat you' ⁴³ So I told you, but you wouldn't listen. Instead, you rebelled against Adonai's order, took matters into your own hands and went up into the hill-country; ⁴⁴ where the Emori living in that hill-country came out against you like bees, defeated you in Se'ir and chased you back all the way to Hormah. ⁴⁵ You returned and cried before Adonai, but Adonai neither listened to what you said nor paid you any attention." (Deuteronomy 1:41-45).

We must follow God's word and be obedient to it. There is punishment if we don't.

¹ "But the people of Isra'el misappropriated some of the goods set aside to be destroyed; for Akhan, the son of Karmi, the son of Zavdi, the son of Zerach, of the tribe of Y'hudah, took some of the things reserved for destruction. In consequence, the

anger of Adonai blazed up against the people of Isra'el" (Joshua 7:1).

⁴ "So from the people about three thousand men went up there, but they were routed by the men of Ai.

⁵ The men of Ai killed some 36 of them and chased them from before their gate all the way to Sh'varim (Shebarim), attacking them on the descent. The hearts of the people melted and turned to water" (Joshua 7:4-5).

I must end with Deuteronomy 20:1-4:

¹ "When you go out to fight your enemies and see horses, chariots and a force larger than yours, **you are not to be afraid of them; because Adonai your God, who brought you up from the land of Egypt, is with you.**

² When you are about to go into battle, the Cohen is to come forward and address the people.

³ He should tell them, '**Listen Isra'el! You are about to do battle against your enemies. Don't be fainthearted or afraid; don't be alarmed or frightened by them;**

Everything goes back to Gan-Eden (the Garden)

⁴ because ADONAI YOUR GOD IS GOING WITH YOU TO FIGHT ON YOUR BEHALF AGAINST YOUR ENEMIES AND GIVE YOU VICTORY.'"

Father, we cannot even breathe on our own. As the Hebrew children in the desert found out, it is all by Your grace and mercy that we live and have our being. So we thank you for going before us and preparing the way.

Chapter 4

Abba's Words, His Voice

---◇---

Our Abba's words are life, for there is much power in His Word. All He needs to do is speak and His will happens in the physical and spiritual world, with the exception of our relationship with Him. To us He gave free will. Some nonbelievers think this was a mistake, but it was not, it was a sign of and a wonderful gift given to us out of Abba's love.

1 Kings 19:11-12 is a portion of the story of Elijah, Jezebel and the prophets of baal:

[11] "He said, "Go outside, and stand on the mountain before Adonai"; and right then and there, Adonai went past. A mighty blast of wind tore the mountains apart and broke the rocks in pieces before Adonai, but Adonai was not in the wind. After the

wind came an earthquake, but Adonai was not in the earthquake.

¹² After the earthquake, fire broke out; but Adonai was not in the fire. And after the fire **came a quiet, subdued voice."**

He speaks to us in a still small voice. We may choose to ignore that still small voice, or follow it, that is our decision, our choice made of our own free will, from a gift given to us by a loving Father. This is an extremely important truth in creation and redemption. In creation, God spoke and it HAPPENED! Light did not say, "No! I do not want to be," **IT WAS**! There was no free will. Light had no option, it was subject to and obedient to God, as was all of creation. He told the seas they could only go so far.

²⁹ "*When He prescribed boundaries for the sea,* ***so that its water would not transgress His command****, when He marked out the foundations of the earth."* (Proverbs 8:29).

²² *"Don't you fear me?–says Adonai. Won't you tremble at my presence?* ***I made the shore the limit for the sea; by eternal decree it cannot pass****. Its

waves may toss, but to no avail; although they roar, they cannot cross it" (Jeremiah 5:22).

All of creation was subject to and obedient to God, except in the case of man. Abba gave man freewill so we could be true worshippers and learn to love. We are able to have a deeper level of fellowship with God because of freewill. He desires our willful fellowship and worship of Him. Freewill is, I believe, one of God's greatest gifts. The greatest, of course, being salvation, redemption, the life of His Son, the shedding of the Messiah's blood for our redemption and restoration to Abba, for the atonement of our sins. If it were not for the atonement of our sinful life, we could not have fellowship with Abba. More correctly stated, Abba could not have fellowship with us because of our filth, our sin. Yahweh provided a way for this to happen through Messiah Yeshua's death and resurrection.

There is much freedom in true love. God could have made all people alike in their worship of Him, but that is not love, nor would it be true worship. The best way I can describe it would be to compare two groups of people. In one group you have twenty people who love God and worship Him with all their hearts, minds, bodies and souls. In the other there are 1000 people in almost robotic worship. There is no **heartfelt** praise, no love, it is barren and seems empty. It is lacking depth of love and freedom. Where would you rather be?

Abba desires a people who want to serve Him, be with Him, follow Him, love Him, worship Him, trust Him... In this love comes God's biggest miracle of all, His gift of salvation, restoration, and redemption by man's humblest act of repentance and acceptance of God's free gift. Remember, in creation there was total obedience, but in redemption, God has to deal with man's free will. He will not force man to follow Him that would go against His love. He has to deal with man's free will and let man decide his own fate, which is truly based upon a free and loving relationship with our heavenly Father.

In His creation He reveals Himself, reveals His nature for us to see. God says He has placed the knowledge of Himself in each man. Prior to the indwelling of the Holy Spirit in man, the knowledge of God was seen in His creation and in His mighty acts for and towards His people, the Hebrew children. I say towards because He is a loving father and bestows good gifts and chastisement and punishment upon His children as well.

Father, We thank you for your gift of life, of love, of chastisement, of sacrifice, of atonement, of restoration, and for fellowship.

Chapter 5

Abba's Plan, His Way

―――――∝―――――

The nation of Israel was born out of slavery, out of captivity in the land of Egypt, in Goshen. If it weren't for the captivity and the Hebrew slaves being kept in a Ghetto, they would have most likely assimilated into the Egyptian culture and would not have become the Jewish people. It was through the 430 years in Egypt, the experience in captivity, and in the desert that God chose to make Himself known to the world by bringing to fruition His plan, by establishing in captivity the Jewish people. His chosen ones and then setting them free and leading them into the promised land through the desert experience, making the nation of Israel.

Our walk on the Highway of Holiness mimics their path of bondage to redemption and to salvation. A major difference though is the indwelling of the Holy Spirit in us. The Hebrews wandering in the desert did not have this wondrous gift from Abba. When I think about how difficult it is today to live the "believer's" life with His help and leading, I am amazed that they were able to do what they did. I know in my own life how miserably I fail at times with the indwelling presence of the Holy Spirit. How would I do without His presence in my day to day life?

The physical land of Israel was chosen by God for the world to physically see and be reminded of what God did for His Chosen People: to show His power and might, His love, His deliverance, His salvation. If you lived in Asia, the Middle East, or Africa, the land of Israel was on your journey from one to the other. So when people passed through Israel, they were face to face with God's people and His mighty acts, face to face with His love, grace, and goodness, and His punishments towards His people. This is so very important, the power of His love and mercy towards those who follow Him. The desert wandering is filled with so many stories of

His faithfulness, His power, His chastisement, His redemption, and His love.

The understanding that God chose and made the nation of Israel, this belief, the trust in this truth is foundational to our faith, to our understanding of who Yahweh is. God is a covenantal God and is a faithful keeper of His Word, of His covenant. When God makes a change to a covenant, He tells us. He does not make a change and then expect us to guess what the change was. If He is not faithful to His Word, then we have **zero assurances**! We must trust and believe Him here to be able to move on in our walk. We must wean ourselves from the milk and move to solid food. For if we do not understand or trust this truth, once again, we have no foundation for anything else He says. **If this isn't true, what else is false?**

It is actually difficult to read the Tanakh without reading on every page some aspect of who God is. He reveals an aspect of Himself on almost every page. I do not mean you have to look for it and read into the scripture to find it; He has it clearly delineated in His Word. Something about who He is, something He did or will do, something about Him personally.

Father, reveal more of yourself to us as we draw closer to you, more of you and less of us.

Chapter 6

The Path We Choose to Walk

———∝———

We must understand that our God has a path for us to walk, and if you think about a path, paved or not, it is easier to walk on the path than through the briar and rocks. Get off that path and the journey becomes a much more arduous journey. The accuser ALWAYS has his counterfeit to God, so he also has a path for us to walk along. So in walking out our life on Earth, we have two choices: we either walk the path God has laid out for us, or we walk the path the accuser has for us. There is not a third choice, a third path.

That path is described in Isaiah 35:8-10:

⁸ *"A highway will be there, a way, called the* **Highway of Holiness***, The unclean will not pass*

The Path We Choose to Walk

over it, but it will be for those whom He guides- fools will not stray along it.

⁹ No lion or other beast of prey will be there, traveling on it. They will not be found there, but the redeemed will go there.

¹⁰ Those ransomed by Adonai will return and come with singing to Tziyon (Zion), on their heads will be everlasting joy. They will acquire gladness and joy, while sorrow and sighing will flee". Our Highway of Holiness."

I think a lot of people believe there is a third neutral path, a path that is neither God's path nor satan's path, just one that is neither. There are but two paths and we are either serving God in our actions or we are serving satan. There is not a third path, a third option or choice.

It is our Abba's intent we walk His Highway, His path to follow Him, obeying Him, trusting Him. It is not a broad road; one cannot veer to the right or left too much. This Highway is very well defined by the Word.

In the book of Mark, chapter 10:31, Yeshua says in reference to the Kingdom in the last days:

31 "Many who are first will be last, and many who are last will be first."

In other words, here on Earth we see many believers, leaders whom we look to as just that, leaders of the faith, but they may have some aspect of their walk, their teaching, something which is not pleasing to God. Remember, it is not our path, it is His path, His way, by His design not ours. An important thing to remember is that, He does not change, we do.

17 "every good act of giving and every perfect gift is from above, coming down from the Father who made the Heavenly lights; with Him there is neither variation nor darkness caused by turning" (James 1:17).

8 "Yeshua the Messiah is the same yesterday, today and forever" (Hebrews 13:8). **MAN IS THE VARIABLE! IT IS ALWAYS US! NEVER OUR HEAVENLY FATHER**

105 "Your Word is a lamp for my foot and light on my path." (Psalm 119:105).

There is no map from the local store, no GPS, only God's Word as a guide for this path. It is His path, His way. What we do on Earth does not change who He is or His plan. The only change our behavior effects on Earth is the timing of His plan, it does not change His plan, only the timing. God began His plan at the garden and has had a few iterations from then until now, but all with the same intent: Fellowship on a face to face basis, Redemption, Restoration and face to face Fellowship again. I imagine it as though God has a huge hourglass and at the garden, at man's fall, He turned that hourglass up and the sand began to flow. When man is following him it is turned onto its side and not flowing, but when man is in a degenerate state, it is set upright and the sand begins to flow. During Noah's day, it ran out and after the flood it was turned on its side again, to begin another saga.

[14] *"Then, if my people, who bear my name, will humble themselves, pray, seek my face and turn from their evil ways, I will hear from heaven, forgive their sin and heal their land"* (2 Chronicles 7:14). Our repentance and prayers can hold back God's vengeance for a season.

We can read in Genesis chapters 6-8, the account of the flood. In Genesis 6:13

[13] "God said to Noach (Noah), 'The end of all living beings has come before Me, for because of them the earth is filled with violence. I will destroy them along with the earth.'"

We see that God has had His fill with man's evilness and decided to end all life with the exception of a few, Noah and his family and the animals saved on the ark. We can read the story of Sodom and Gomorrah in Genesis chapters 18 and 19, how God had His fill and decided to destroy them. In these instances we see God's Holiness, His righteousness, and His judgment.

Now in the book of Jonah, we also have a story about Nineveh, Jonah, and a big fish, and how one man at the urging and leading of God caused a nation to repent. Abba spared that nation. Here we see clearly the loving side of the father, His heart of love for His repentant children. I believe we can say the same about all three stories. All three show His loving heart and at the same time His Righteousness, Holiness, judgment, and His love for His children.

The Path We Choose to Walk

Remember, God wanted the world to see Himself through the nation of Israel, through His people, in order for them to be drawn to Him. Even in chastisement Abba is showing us His love, His care, His concern over His children. For what father does not, in love, chastise his children to bring them to right thinking. We can read and see His love through these lessons, through His actions, which are all meant to draw us to Him, not away from Him. In these lessons we can see Him as a just Father, a loving Father, a caring Father, and a Holy Father.

Father, your Word tells us that "Thy word is a lamp unto thy feet and a light unto thy path". May we walk on your path not veering to the right or left, but may we follow your light to your Holiness.

Chapter 7

Returning to a Church Prepared and Our Warnings

———⸺✕⸺———

God says, and this is my paraphrase, "I am returning to a Church prepared, I am not returning to prepare a Church." This is a very important principle for us to let permeate our souls. He is not returning to prepare the church, but to a church prepared:

> [35] "Be dressed for action and have your lamp lit,
> [36] like people waiting for their master's return after a wedding feast; so that when he comes and knocks, they will open the door for him without delay.
> [37] Happy the slaves whom the master finds alert when he comes! Yes! I tell you he will put on his

work clothes, seat them at the table, and come serve them himself!

³⁸ *Whether it is late at night or early in the morning, if this is how he finds them, those slaves are happy.*

³⁹ *But notice this: no house-owner would let his house be broken into if he knew when the thief was coming.*

⁴⁰ *You too, be ready! For the Son of Man will come when you are not expecting Him"* (Luke 12:35-40).

² *"because you yourselves well know that the Day of the Lord will come like a thief in the night.*

³ *When people are saying, 'Everything is so peaceful and secure,' then destruction will suddenly come upon them, the way labor pains come upon a pregnant woman, and there is no way they will escape"* (1 Thessalonians 5:2-3).

When He returns, there is not a grace period to prepare, you must be ready! We must turn to Revelations and look at the warnings to the 7 churches, the 7 spiritual states of man. These warnings are our checklist, our guide to compare our spiritual state to.

EVERY BELIEVER and CHURCH FALLS INTO ONE or MORE OF THE SEVEN CHURCHES! There is not an unspecified or hidden eighth church. We all fall into one of the seven and not all believers are of the churches of Philadelphia or Smyrna. It is important that each of us as individuals and corporately as a body check our walks against the Word of God. If we all fell into those two, there would be no need for the warnings to the other five churches; Warnings with dire consequences!

We may have one, two, three, or all of these failings in our walk, in our relationship with Abba, for these are spiritual states. The warnings are our spiritual GPS, (God's Positioning System), for our walk with Him.

Remember what Yeshua said in Matthew 7:13-14:

[13] "Go in through the narrow gate; for the gate that leads to destruction is wide and the road broad, and many travel it;

[14] but it is a narrow gate and a hard road that leads to life, and only a few find it."

If we are on the wrong path, Abba's GPS reroutes us to the correct path, God's path, His Highway of Holiness. If we find ourselves in one of these states we must adjust our walk. He does not adjust or reroute the path. He reroutes us to get us back on track, but it is we who must change not Him. It is on His terms not ours. We are in no position to dictate the terms of salvation, the terms of His plan. There is only one way...His way, through the Blood of the Lamb, our savior Yeshua the Messiah.

Abba, open our eyes, ears, and hearts to You. Help us to see the spiritual state we are in. Right us and guide us to Your truth.

CHAPTER 8

Man's Dominion and Decision (We Must Choose II)

---—∝—---

In the garden God gave man dominion over the Earth and all it contained. He made man's "help meet" physically out of man. The garden was the original church. You had God, the Creator of all that is, "walking" with the first man and woman in the evening in the garden. God fellowshipped with them, spoke with them.

This was Father's original plan. His original intent was to have fellowship with us, to have intimacy with us. Through this original model we can see Abba's heart towards mankind. His desire to walk with man, to have closeness, that one-on-one fellowship. This model is also the model for all relationships, the only

Man's Dominion and Decision (We Must Choose II)

difference is the relationship itself: husband to wife, child to parent, sibling to sibling, business owner to employees, etc. All relationships stem from this model, the garden.

I do not need to tell you it did not work as Abba planned. Man has always had free will, again, this also shows Abba's heart, His love towards His creation. He desires that we **"choose"** to trust Him, we **"choose"** to love Him, we **"choose"** to worship Him, and we **"choose"** to follow Him for who He is.

Throughout the Old Covenant we see this time and time again where Father displays His heart, His desire, His intent towards man. Again it is almost impossible to go one page without His heart being shown to man in His Word. Time after time He is telling us, showing us His heart, His desire to communicate His plan for us, His intent towards us.

It was my intent to list some examples here from the bible, but I felt it more important to just encourage you to literally open your bible to any page and start reading. If you can actually go more than a few pages and not see God revealing Himself to you, a revelation of who He is, I would be shocked. Abba is constantly revealing His nature, His heart,

His love, His judgment, some aspect of Himself on almost every page of His Word!

One aspect of His heart towards us is that He gives us the freedom to choose. We always have the ability to choose right from wrong, His way or the enemies. Our Abba desires a people who will willfully and gladly follow and trust Him, to trust Him as we walk through the desert where food, water... for that matter all aspects of life are arduous. There is nothing easy about a desert experience. Though, through that encounter our faith in Abba can grow stronger and deeper as we see his hand in our experience, as we acknowledge His hand in our lives, as we trust in Him more.

Father, open our hearts to You, show us through Your Word the importance of completely trusting in You.

Chapter 9

Accepting "All" of Life that Comes Our Way

---∝---

One thing that we do not do as sons and daughters is to truly, deeply, completely accept and understand how our life, though at times very painful, has brought us to the place we are in Him today. We must recognize and understand that it was and is the desert and valley experiences that have led us to this point in our walk in Him. Without those experiences, the good in our life, the blessings in our life, and the pain in our life, we might never have arrived at the place we are in Him today. They are, if we allow them, the experiences that draw us to Abba's heart.

Which takes us back to His "Word"; He speaks His Words over us which, when we in our hearts allow them in, are life giving Words. All His love towards us is to bring restoration, so that He may have fellowship with us. Remember, we are born into sin, so we must therefore be restored into Him, a world without sin, for He is sinless.

When we look at the Genesis story our Abba "spoke" this universe into existence. His Words are so powerful, so complete. The Words He speaks over us are even more powerful than the Words of creation. With His children, remember all mankind are His children, there is freedom of choice. Freedom to follow or not to follow, to believe or not to believe, to accept or not to accept. Abba gave us the ability, the freedom to choose. This is one huge aspect of His heart we see every day in our world. Some people follow His lead, His desires for us, and some do the absolute opposite. In restoration, which is truly more miraculous than creation, our will plays a huge role.

Our Father's desire, design, and heart, is that we, through our desert experiences acknowledge and see His love towards us in this and **follow** Him and **trust** Him. Since Abba endowed man with the freedom of choice, this truly makes restoration a miracle bigger than creation. Please understand, creation was and is so beyond incredible, but our repentance and subsequent restoration is even more of a miracle. It requires willful trusting and humble obedience to the Savior!

² "On Shabbat He started to teach in the synagogue, and many who heard Him were astounded. They asked, 'Where did this man get all this? What is this wisdom He has been given? What are these miracles worked through Him?

³ Isn't He just the carpenter? The son of Miryam (Mary)? The brother of Ya'akov (Jacob), Yosi (Joseph), Y'hudah (Judah) and Shim'on (Simon)? Aren't His sisters here with us?' And they took offense at Him.

⁴ But Yeshua said to them, 'The only place people do not respect a prophet is in his hometown, among his own relatives, and in his own house.'

*⁵ So He could do **NO** miracles there, other than lay His hands on a few sick people and heal them.*

*⁶ **He was amazed at their lack of trust**"* (Mark 6:2-6).

If healing were a bigger miracle than redemption, I believe the Holy Spirit would have chosen Mark's words differently. Instead of the people "hearing" His Words and repenting, they took offense and they lacked the trust in Him as the Messiah. Mark does not mention any repentance on the part of the people.

Abba, we thank You for Your love, for the freedom it brings. We thank You for Your Hand upon our lives, for all that You see us through, for the times You spared us when we were not even aware.

Chapter 10

The Father's Constant Heart and Our Opportunities to Grow

―――――∝―――――

Man is fallible and God understands this all too well, but I believe in this, He loves us more. It makes very obvious our need for Him, for Him in our daily lives to talk with, to ask for forgiveness, to ask for help, to ask for knowledge, wisdom, etc. What father does not want to be needed by his children? What father does not want to be a part of his children's lives, to be "there" for them in everything? Well, our Heavenly Abba is just that, he is **always there, always!**

We must remember, there are no "shazams" with God...none. If I were able to take you now to the highest mountain tops, the one thing they would all have in common is the complete and total lack of life. Nothing grows on the top of the mountain. There is exhilaration being on the top, with an incredible view, but the best growth takes place in the valley. It is in the valley where we grow, where we draw close to, where we hear our Father's heartbeat. When we are there it can be somewhat painful, but when we come out the other side there is incredible joy and growth beyond measure.

Our Abba uses the difficult, painful experiences in our life to help us grow, to draw us closer to Him. He allows us to experience the pain and through Him come out on top. In having said this, it is still our will to acknowledge and see the experience as growth, or worse, to become hard and bitter and lose sight of what is truly important: growth of deeper roots, growth of a deeper understanding, growth of deeper trust in Abba, having that confidence, that deeper trust in Him. Repentance and restoration comes through our inner man yielding to Abba. Again, restoration is a **HUGE** miracle!

[5] *"And He could do no miracle there except that He laid His hands on a few sick people and healed them"* (Mark 6:5).

The Father's Constant Heart and Our Opportunities to Grow

We can see Yeshua's love towards us in all these experiences or we can become hard, bitter, and hateful. That is our choice, our decision. The Old Covenant is filled with this principle. The law was given on the mountain top to the people in the valley, the desert. This concept, when not fought, and is, in fact, embraced, will affect much growth.

Try this no matter the situation you find yourselves in. The next time you do, think, or say something you know is wrong— saying or thinking something derogatory about one of His creation— ask Abba for forgiveness. Truly repent and ask Him to let you walk through that trial again. Trust me, He will give you the opportunity to literally walk this out 20 times in a day. I know, I've counted. Had I been really difficult, really hard headed, it would have exceeded 20 times. LOL.

Abba is faithful to forgive and to afford us the opportunity to grow in Him, to walk through these situations of growth in Him again, and again. He really is faithful. Abba's desire for us is growth in Him. Sometimes we "pass the test" and sometimes we fail miserably, but Abba is always there. When you fail, repent and ask God to give you another opportunity to walk through that again so that you may "pass" the test. He will, for He is faithful, even up to 7 times 70. Ask Him, welcome the trial as it truly is for your good, for your growth, a lesson coming from a loving, caring father.

Daniel 11:32 states:

*[32] "Those who act wickedly against the covenant he will corrupt with His blandishments, **but the people who know their God "will stand firm and prevail"***. This is a very powerful scripture and a promise. Though we must recognize that not all promises are present, some are future.

Father your Word is life and nourishment for our soul. Give us the opportunity to grow in you, to live the life you have planned for us. Walk with us through the valley; Abba we submit and commit our lives to you.

Chapter 11

We Must Choose III

In all of life there are but two paths we walk: we are either on the *Highway of Holiness,* walking with our Father, or we walk the path the accuser wants us to walk. There is not a third neutral path, just as there is not a third entity. There was from the beginning, prior to the rebellion, only God and His heavenly host. After the fall we now have Abba and the accuser, there is not a third party or a third way. If we think of our walk, our life in this way, it becomes clearer in our decision making, for our life is a life of choices. Every day we make decisions, not all decisions have the same impact; what color socks should I wear, which dress, which tie? Should I eat eggs and toast, or just toast?

In having said this we should still in our day to day life be sensitive to the leading of the Holy Spirit in **all our decisions**. As we allow, and it is our decision, the Holy Spirit to lead us, He will. He will lead us to places we may never have intended to go that day. Or Have us do things we never thought possible or never thought on our own to do. He will guide us to His **"divine appointments,"** place us where He needs us; and, by the way, we do not need to be given an itinerary, or be given the reason why. All we need be is open and obedient to His leading. Remember more of Abba and less of us.

Our walk with Abba, led by the Holy Spirit, will affect change in the lives of the people around us, for Abba's presence is life changing. He leads us to His divine appointments as we allow Him to live in us and lead us. An example: you are going out to lunch, so, a decision must be made about where to eat. Abba may very well have a divine appointment for an encounter, a divine appointment with someone for that meeting to impact, to touch another person who is in need of a kind face, an act of kindness, a simple word, etc. We may be hungry for Mexican, but today the Holy Spirit says we have to eat Thai.

[24] *"Moreover, those who belong to the Messiah Yeshua have put their old nature to death on the stake, along with its passions and desires.*
[25] *Since it is through the Spirit that we have Life, let it also be through the Spirit that **we order our lives day by day**"* (Galatians 5:24-25).

As we walk out our life, allowing Him to live His life in us, we will have many such divine appointments. These are His way of loving His children, filling their needs, emotional, financial, physical, spiritual, etc.

It is in our obedience to Him where He is seen in our physical world. Just as where He physically placed Eretz Israel for the world to see and to be touched by them, we become this same thing, macro and micro. Eretz Israel is macro and we are micro. We are there for the world to see Him in us. The world does not see us in Him, but they see God in us, in our actions, our obedience. They see His actions taking us from Egypt to the Promise Land.

Abba, More of you and less of us.

Chapter 12

This Body is only Temporary (a wonderful blessing from Abba)

———⋈———

Our physical bodies are made from the earth and at present are subject to the earth and its spiritual and physical laws, for we are born into a world of sin. When we die to self and are born again, only our physical bodies are subject to this world, but our spirit is forever and is not subject to this earth or the accuser anymore. We have forgiveness from our sins when we are **"born again."** Sin no longer rules over us because we have atonement through Messiah Yeshua's death on the cross, which brought us into fellowship with Abba.

[7] *"If you are doing what is good, shouldn't you hold your head high? And if you don't do what is*

This Body is only Temporary(a wonderful blessing from Abba)

*good, sin is crouching at the door- it wants you, **but you can rule over it***" (Genesis 4:7).

Now we may live a life for Him. His work on the cross is our salvation, His resurrection is our guarantee, and His ascension is our strength. Without His ascension we would not have the Holy Spirit. Without the Holy Spirit we would be virtually powerless and alone, but through Yeshua's ascension we have the gift of the Holy Spirit dwelling in us, guiding us, speaking to us, and comforting us.

We have the Almighty, our Abba, the creator of **EVERYTHING, alive in us**!!! What a glorious thought, what a comforting thought. Remember, in the Garden Yahweh came to Adam and Eve and fellowshipped with them, walked with them. He came to them because that is where His heart was. Once they fell, you do not read of such encounters, but Abba's heart was always and is always towards His children, so is His desire to have time with us. Children of the living God, understand and let this truth become who you are, let it burn so deep within you, let it permeate every atom of your being. You are His and He loves you so, so much more than we can comprehend. **HE WILL NEVER LEAVE YOU OR FORSAKE YOU.**

We need to understand the depth of His love and His desire to fellowship with us, for He made a plan to be able to do this once again; another step towards the Garden, via the Holy Spirit. The indwelling of the Holy Spirit at Shavu'ot was Yahweh coming to have fellowship with us again, to walk with us, to be with us. Though it is not face to face, it is the next to last step before we will see Him face to face!! Wow!!!! Do you see and understand the depth of His love for you? He did this for you!! He desired to be with you so much He sent His Son to cleanse you and His Holy Spirit to live in you.

It is we who leave Him, it is we who make a mockery of the life He gave us to live. No matter our circumstance, no matter our situation, no matter how dire, our Abba is there with us; Always and forever. Abba's love, " a'ha'va," is love without expectation. It is love for love's sake, not for what you can do for Him, but for whom you are, His child. Even we love our children this way, so why would we think differently of our Heavenly Father?

Abba, in this life you have given us, may we recognize that you love us beyond anything we can

This Body is only Temporary(a wonderful blessing from Abba)

understand and your desire is to be with us. As we submit our lives to You, we are used by You to be Your hands and feet, to be a witness for your lost children of this most precious gift, Your love! Your Salvation!!

Chapter 13

Always Follow and Trust Abba, It is All for our Good!

---------∝---------

Often times when we are called by God to do something, whatever it may be, we must be careful to not "make it happen," it being our doing not His. The end result may be the similar, but it may not be the same. It will be through us that it happens and not through Him. It was our doing, our way, not His. The result for that specific thing may be similar or the same, but something may have been lost somewhere in the process. A person, whose life God wanted to touch, may be passed over. For it should always be His way through the entire process. Remember, Abba gave us an example, the Hebrew children in the desert. Abba "always" went before them, always provided food, water, safety, etc. It was always His provision. He is no different today,

⁸"Yeshua the Messiah is the same, yesterday, today and forever!" (Hebrews 13:8).

Again, Jeremiah 29:11 is a great scripture. They are His plans, not our plans. I would like to add this truth of God here. Abba is not angry with us when we act when we believe we are hearing from the Holy Spirit, but we are in error. Abba would much rather we do something than nothing. In the parable of the talents God was not pleased with the servant who buried his talent.

Now remember, there is a difference in doing something you clearly know is wrong, something that goes against His Word, and doing something you truly think you should do. When we think about the way Yeshua taught us to pray:

⁷ "And when you pray, don't babble on and on like the pagans, who think God will hear them better if they talk a lot.

⁸ Don't be like them, because your Father knows what you need before you ask Him.

⁹ *You, therefore pray like this:*
'Our Father in heaven!
   May your name be kept Holy,
¹⁰ *May your Kingdom come,*
   *Your will be done on earth as **it is** in Heaven.*
¹¹ *Give us the food we need today,*
¹² *Forgive us what we have done wrong,*
   As we too have forgiven those who have wronged us.
¹³ *And do not lead us into hard testing,*
   But keep us safe from the evil one.
   *For kingship, power and glory are yours forever'" (Matthew 6:7-13).
(* The latter half of verse 13 is not found in the oldest manuscripts)

Can you see those two simple words **"it is?"** **"It is"** is very definite. "It may" or "it might," are not so definite. Yeshua is telling us it is all about His perfect plan, all about His perfect will, all about His perfect desire for us. His perfect plan has been planned out and **"is in"** Heaven, if you will, waiting for us to submit to it. Personally, the thought of this surrender to His perfect will, His perfect plan, perfect desire for me, gives such peace, such joy to my soul. Why would I not want to be in that place with Him?

The other truth in this matter is that our Abba's Words, words so powerful, can take our mess and what the enemy meant for harm and turn it into something good.

[19] "*But Yosef (Joseph) said to them, 'Don't be afraid!- am I in the place of God?*
[20] *You meant to do me harm, but God meant it for good- so that it would come about as it is today, with many people's lives being saved'*" (Genesis 50:19-20).

[28] "*Furthermore, we know that God causes everything to work together for the good of those who love God and are called in accordance with His purpose*" (Romans 8:28).

One great example of this would be the "Spanish Inquisition." What King Ferdinand and Queen Isabella meant for harm, our God turned into good! The Jews were forced out of Spain, made to leave all valuables behind, and, some people believe, it was partly this money that enabled Spain to fund Columbus for his voyage. Also, this was an opening

Let me introduce you to my Abba

for only the second nation in the history of the world that was founded upon God, to be brought into existence. People can rewrite history all they want, but it does not change the facts!

Abba, We, your true Church, rest in knowing that You are **IN CONTROL**!! We stand and rest in You, in the peace and joy this brings us.

Chapter 14

Change is Painful, But it Does Not Have to be

———⚯———

God gives warnings to His people throughout the Tanakh (Old Covenant) and I believe we often overlook these warnings. We think of them as to Israel only, or at least, we do not see ourselves in these sinful states. We should not forget that God made provision, even then, for the gentile in **all** of what Israel was to do, and was to become. The gentile was there from the Passover, to the wandering, to the entering into the promised land, to salvation. We are a part of Israel today, adopted, grafted in, which is a truth so often overlooked by the church.

¹⁶ "Now if the challah (dough) offered as first fruits is holy, so is the whole loaf. And if the root is holy, so are the branches.

¹⁷ But if some of the branches were broken off, and you- a wild olive–were grafted in among them and have become **equal** sharers in the rich root of the olive tree,

¹⁸ then don't boast as if you were better than the branches! However, if you do boast, remember that you are not supporting the root, the root is supporting you.

¹⁹ So you will say, 'Branches were broken off so that I might be grafted in.'

²⁰ True, but so what? They were broken off because of their lack of trust. However, you keep your place only because of your trust. So don't be arrogant; on the contrary, be terrified!

²¹ For if God did not spare the natural branches, He certainly won't spare you!

²² So take a good look at God's kindness and His severity: on the one hand, severity toward those who fell off; but on the other hand, God's kindness towards you–provided you maintain yourself in that kindness! Otherwise, you too will be cut off!

²³ *Moreover, the others, if they do not persist in their lack of trust, will be grafted back in.*
²⁴ *For if you were cut out of what is by nature a wild olive tree and grafted, contrary to nature, into a cultivated olive tree, how much more will these natural branches be grafted back into their own olive tree!"* (Romans 11:16-24).

After Messiah's death, resurrection, and ascension, the gentile is now an adopted child, grafted into the Jewish root of Messiah, a rightful heir! The gentile is not a replacement, but a fellow heir. God has not abandoned Israel, He has not replaced Israel, and his covenant is forever. He just made provision for all people to enter into fellowship with Him, into His family.

²⁷ *"My Father has handed over everything to Me. Indeed, no one fully knows the Son except the Father, and no one fully knows the Father except the Son and those to whom the Son wishes to reveal Him"* (Matthew 11:27).

This was to allow all to become a part of His people, to be His chosen people with Israel. This is so very important to understand, to accept as a truth from God's Word. The accuser sees and understands this as is seen in his war on God's people, for it includes the church. In any battle, physical or spiritual, the tenet "Divide and Conquer" is true. Today, the Body of the Messiah has been divided by the accuser. God's church is one body and one bride or Bridesmaid! Nowhere in the Word is there a description of two bodies or two Bride's or Bridesmaids. In fact, the only time you hear of two is in the story of the preparation of the **Bridesmaids** for **the Groom.** The Bridesmaids are broken down into two groups where one group is prepared and the other is not.

¹ "The Kingdom of Heaven at that time will be like ten bridesmaids who took their lamps and went out to meet the Groom.

² Five of them were foolish and five were sensible.

³ The foolish ones took lamps with them but no oil,

⁴ whereas the others took flasks of oil with their lamps.

⁵ Now the Bridegroom was late, so they all went to sleep.

⁶ It was in the middle of the night that the cry rang out, 'The Bridegroom is here! Go out to meet Him!'

7 The girls all woke up and prepared their lamps for lighting.

8 The foolish ones said to the sensible ones, 'Give us some of your oil, because our lamps are going out.'

9 'No,' they replied, 'there may not be enough for both you and us. Go to the oil dealers and buy some for yourselves.'

10 But as they were going off to buy, the Bridegroom came. Those who were ready went with Him to the wedding feast, and the door was shut.

11 Later, the other bridesmaids came. 'Sir! Sir!' they cried, 'Let us in!'

12 But He answered, 'Indeed! 'I tell you, I don't know you!'

13 So stay alert, because you know neither the day nor the hour" (Matthew 25:1-13).

Ephesians is some of the best writing to establish and confirm this in God. It is written to the Gentile converts in Ephesus. Please read all of Ephesians, for it is a wonderful faith building letter. I want to start at the end of Ephesians 1:22-23, and continue through 2:1-22:

²² "Also, He put all things under His feet and made Him head over everything for the Messianic Community,

²³ which is His body, the full expression of Him who fills all creation."

¹ "You used to be dead because of your sins and acts of disobedience.

² You walked in the ways of the 'olam hazeh (this world, this age) and obeyed the ruler of the powers of the air, who is still at work among the disobedient.

³ Indeed, we all once lived this way- we followed the passions of our old nature and obeyed the wishes of our old nature and our own thoughts. In our natural condition we were headed for God's wrath, just like everyone else.

⁴ But God who is so rich in mercy and loves us with such intense love

⁵ that, even when we were dead because of our acts of disobedience, He brought us to life along with the Messiah- it is by grace that you have been delivered.

⁶ That is, God raised us up with the Messiah Yeshua and seated us with Him in heaven,

⁷ in order to exhibit in the ages to come how infinitely rich is His grace, how great is His kindness toward us who are united with the Messiah Yeshua.

⁸ for you have been delivered by grace through trusting, and even this is not your accomplishment but God's gift.

⁹ You were not delivered by your own actions; therefore no one should boast,

¹⁰ For we are of God's making, created in union with the Messiah Yeshua for a life of good actions already prepared by God for us to do.

*¹¹ **Therefore remember your former state: you Gentiles by birth-** called the Uncircumcised by those who, merely because of an operation on their flesh, are called the Circumcised-*

*¹² at that time had no Messiah. **You were ESTRANGED from the NATIONAL LIFE of Isra'el.** You were foreigners to the covenants embodying God's promise. You were in this world without hope and without God.*

*¹³ **But now, you who were once far off have been brought near** through the shedding of the Messiah's blood.*

*¹⁴ For He Himself is our Shalom- **He has made us both one and has broken down the m'chitzah***

which divided us (divider which separates people into two groups, the fence which separates the inner parts of the Temple, where only Jews could enter from the court of the Gentiles)

[15] by destroying in His own body the enmity occasioned by the Torah, with its commands set forth in the forms of ordinances. **He did this in order to create in union with Himself from the two groups a single new humanity** and thus make shalom,

[16] and in order to reconcile to God **BOTH IN A SINGLE BODY** by being executed on a stake as a criminal and **thus killing in Himself the enmity.**

[17] Also, when He came, He announced as Good News shalom to you far off and shalom to those nearby,

[18] news that through Him we both have access in one Spirit to the Father.

[19] **So then, you are no longer foreigners and strangers. On the contrary, you are fellow-citizens with God's people and members of God's family.**

[20] You have built on the the foundation of the emissaries and the prophets, with the Cornerstone being Yeshua the Messiah himself.

²¹ *In union with Him the whole building is held together, and it is growing into a holy temple in union with the Lord.*

²² *Yes, in union with Him, you yourselves are being built together into a spiritual dwelling-place for God!"*

I believe Exodus 12:48 is prophetic in reference to the Gentile being made an equal sharer with the Jew in the body of the Messiah, a member of the church, the bride of Messiah:

⁴⁸ *"If a foreigner staying with you wants to observe Adonai's Pesach, all his males must be circumcised. Then he may take part and observe it;* ***he will be like a citizen of the land. But no uncircumcised person is to eat it."***

This scripture goes hand in hand with Ephesians and when you think about the scriptures in Romans that talk about circumcision. We know true circumcision is of the heart. In Exodus, in the King James Version, the word in place of foreigner is "stranger," which means sojourner. This stranger shall be as one born in the land. He ***"will be like a citizen of the*** *land."* The Webster definition of Citizen is "an inhabitant of a city or town, especially one entitled to the rights and privileges of a freeman. A member of a state; a native or naturalized person who owes allegiance to a government and is entitled to protection from it."

Acts 15 is an often used book and chapter to make the case for the separation of the Jewish believer and Gentile convert in the early church. It was never God's intent to have "**any division**" in His bride and I do not believe this was in any way meant to be a division amongst the early church. The whole dispute started, because there were those who believed the converts should be circumcised and keep the Torah, all of it. Early teaching clearly refutes this idea, for they walked in freedom and true circumcision is of the heart.

Yeshua Himself came and said, "He was not doing away with Torah," but, in fact, made Torah an issue of the heart and said "He came to complete it." I in no way believe, or am I saying, they or we are under the law, but rather that portion of the Law that has no effect on redemption since Yeshua's death on the cross. Circumcision, eating kosher, the ceremonial washing of hands, the sacrificial system, etc... Those things were buried by Messiah on the cross and at His death. All of the Torah that deals with man's actions that are related to his heart are still valid, still in place, but on a much tougher basis; they are no longer action sins, but mere thoughts. Murder, adultery, etc. The difference now is that we have Jesus as our Paschal Lamb.

The Gentile believers were given four commands: abstain from what has been sacrificed to idols, from blood, from things strangled and from fornication. These prohibitions for the Gentiles were, if you will, issues from the life they lived in the past. The "Pagans" lived a life of Idol worship, sacrifice to those idols, using blood in cooking and were very much into fornication. As far as strangulation; God loves all of His creation and even though He has given man dominion over it and has given us animals to eat, there is an expectation from God that we are to be respectful of what we do with them, which includes their killing for our food.

Father, help us to see Your heart and be submissive to You and Your plan, and to rid our lives of the things we hold onto from our past that are not pleasing to you.

Chapter 15

Let's Revisit the Warnings (II) Again, and Some More Change (Pain II)

———∝———

We really need to take a look at the warnings to the churches in Revelations. For many years I was so confused in reading portions of the warnings to the churches of Smyrna and Philadelphia.

⁹ *"I know how you are suffering and how poor you are (though in fact you are rich!), and **I know the insults of those who call themselves Jews but aren't**–on the contrary, they are a synagogue of the adversary"* (Revelations 2:9).

⁹ *"Here I will give you some from the synagogue of the adversary, **those who call themselves Jews but aren't**–on the contrary, they are lying–see, I will*

cause them to come and prostrate themselves at your feet, and they will know that I have loved you" (Revelations 3:9).

Here we have John being given words in reference to people "**in**" the church who call themselves Jews, but who are not. Taking these simple words and applying them to the church, they are truly meaningless. What is the significance of anyone saying they are Jewish, but they are really Spanish, Italian, French, Polish, Baptist, Catholic, non-denominational? It does not cause anyone any physical, mental, or spiritual harm or problems. The only issue is one of deception and it's deception without significance. It is just a lie about heritage, which truly affects no one, though it will have an effect on their relationship with Abba, for it is a lie.

Paul in Romans 2:17-29 uses the phrase, "**call yourself a Jew**":

[17] *"But if you **call yourself a Jew** and rest on Torah and boast about God*

[18] *and know His will and give your approval to what is right, because you have been instructed from the Torah;*

¹⁹ and if you have persuaded yourself that you are a guide to the blind, a light in the darkness,

²⁰ an instructor for the spiritually unaware and a teacher of children, since in the Torah you have the embodiment of knowledge and truth;

²¹ then, you who teach others, don't you teach yourself? Preaching, **'Thou shalt not steal,'** do you steal?

²² Saying, **'Thou shalt not commit adultery,'** do you commit adultery? Detesting idols, do you commit idolatrous acts?

²³ You who take such pride in Torah, do you, by disobeying the Torah, dishonor God?-

²⁴ as it say's in the Tanakh, **'For it is because of you that God's name is blasphemed by the Goyim.'**

²⁵ For circumcision is indeed of value if you do what the Torah says. But if you are a transgressor of Torah, your circumcision has become uncircumcision!

²⁶ Therefore, if an uncircumcised man keeps the righteous requirements of the Torah, won't his uncircumcision be counted as circumcision?

²⁷ Indeed, the man who is physically uncircumcised but obeys the Torah will stand as a judgment

on you who have had b'rit-milah (circumcision) and have Torah written out, but violate it!

²⁸ For the real Jew is not merely Jewish outwardly: true circumcision is not only external and physical.

²⁹ On the contrary, the real Jew is one inwardly; and true circumcision is of the heart, spiritual not literal; so that his praise comes not from other people but from God."

This is a chastisement and an explanation from Paul referring to hypocritical believers in the body. Those who did not understand God's plan for His people and then ends in a definition of a true believer, a true Jew. In the very next chapter Paul goes on to explain to the adopted sons the significance of the adopted family, the root. We must remember Paul was called to the Gentiles to convert them from paganism to becoming believers in the true God, Messiah Yeshua.

In the letter to the Messianic community in Rome (Romans), Paul says,

¹ "From: Sha'ul, a slave of the Messiah Yeshua, an emissary because I was called and set apart for the Good News of God.

² God promised this Good News in advance through His prophets in the Tanakh.

³ It concerns His Son- He is descended from David physically;

⁴ He was powerfully demonstrated to be Son of God spiritually, set apart by His having been resurrected from the dead; He is Yeshua the Messiah, our Lord.

⁵ Through Him we received grace and were given the work of being an emissary on His behalf promoting trust-grounded obedience among all the Gentiles,

⁶ including you, who have been called by Yeshua the Messiah" (Romans 1:1-6).

Now if you go back to Chapter 14, where Romans 11 is discussed and begin to understand that to a Hebrew speaking person the people in the early church would have been called Jews (because they were) or Messianic (because they were Jews who believed that Yeshua was the Messiah), not Christians. Christian is a Greek word meaning "Christ like," and Christ means "Messiah." Now, with this perspective, when you see the word 'Jew' think 'believer,' and it now makes perfectly good sense. It is all about perspective.

In keeping in the perspective mode, if we think of Jews by birth, believing in and accepting Yeshua as the Messiah, there is no conversion. There is completion!! There is nothing more Jewish than to believe in Yeshua as the Messiah! On the other hand, a Gentile who comes to faith is converted from paganism, atheism, or agnosticism into Yeshua, the Jewish Messiah!!

[16] *"For I am not ashamed of the Good News, since it is God's powerful means of bringing salvation to everyone who keeps on trusting, to the Jew especially, but equally to the Gentile"* (Romans 1:16).

The Jew who does not accept Yeshua is in the same sinking boat as the non-believing gentile.

[9] *"Yes, He will pay back misery and anguish to every human being who does evil, to the Jew first, then to the Gentile"* (Romans 2:9).

What the warning in Revelations is saying is that there are people in the body who are counterfeit. They are sitting in the church building, proclaiming to be Jewish (a Believer/ Messianic), but they are not. They are not following the Word of God, they are, in fact, of the *"synagogue of satan."* Wow! This is a pretty strong indictment of the state of some of the body in the Church.

This is a perfect fit for the scriptures in reference to Revelations and Romans. You must remember the warnings are ***"to the Churches."*** The reference to the people who call *"themselves **'Jews'** and are not,"* are in the body, in the church today! If anyone can tell me of people who are in the church today calling themselves Jews and are not, I would like to meet them. We must meet this scripture head on, we cannot push it off to the side or give it another meaning. **God sees His Church, His Bride as Jewish! It is all about perspective and we need God's!** Again, Abba makes it very clear as we just read in Romans 2.

[28] *"For the real Jew is not merely Jewish outwardly: true circumcision is not only external and physical.*

[29] *On the contrary, the real Jew is one inwardly; and true circumcision is of the heart, spiritual, not literal; so that his praise comes not from other people but from God"* (Romans 2:28-29).

*^{15} "For you did not receive a spirit of slavery to bring you back again into fear; on the contrary, you received the spirit, who **makes us sons** and by whose power we cry out Abba (that is, Dear Father)"* (Romans 8:15).

^{22} "We know that until now, the whole creation has been groaning as with pains of childbirth;

*^{23} and not only it, but we ourselves, who have the first fruits of the Spirit, groan inwardly as we continue waiting eagerly to be **made sons**- that is, to have our whole bodies redeemed and set free"* (Romans 8:22-23).

Remember, God says the Gentile is grafted and adopted into His body, into His people. In adoption the child is no longer a stranger, but a rightful heir! (In these passages the words *makes* and *made* are translated from the Greek word huiŏthĕsia: placing as a son, adoption.) In horticultural grafting you take one plant for its strong roots and the other for its best attributes— its fruit, flowers, etc.— and you insert the tissue of the one into the other; and they grow together as one. Messiah is our root and we are all now fed by the Master as one body.

Think of it from God's perspective: He did not want the Jews to intermarry with the people of the nations before them that they were defeating or driving out.

² *"When He does this, when Adonai your God hands them over ahead of you, and you defeat them, you are to destroy them completely! Do not make any covenant with them. Show them no mercy.*
³ *Don't intermarry with them- don't give your daughter to his son, and don't take his daughter for your son."*
⁴ *For he will turn your children away from following Me in order to serve other gods. If this happens, the anger of Adonai will flare up against you, and He will quickly destroy you"* (Deuteronomy 7:2-4).

If Adonai was so resistant about His people intermarrying: Why would we believe He is any different today? Adonai, "is the same yesterday today and forever". You must remember,,, we are His Bride and He will not allow us to marry out of the faith!!

Abba, unstop the ears, open the eyes, and soften the hearts of Your people so they may see their true heritage that You designed in **YOUR PLAN!!**

Chapter 16

The Church Prepared II

---∝---

In this day we live, the church is being prepared for His return. He will not return to an unprepared church, but a church prepared. He is not returning to prepare a church, but to the church prepared. There are things happening in the world today that are a shaking and sifting. A separation of the sheep and goats is a good analogy.

Having owned goats, I can tell you there is a difference between the two. Goats are independent and will, if left to their own devices, find trouble. If a goat gets out of its pen, he will surely get into trouble, eat the garden, yours or the neighbors or the neighbor's neighbor... They will not wander off in a group but will head in many different directions.

It is their nature. Even Yeshua understood this very clearly when He tells the story about the separation of the sheep and goats. He chooses these animals because of their inherent differences, that nature that was built into them from the beginning.

> [32] *"All the nations will be assembled before Him, and He will separate people one from another as a shepherd separates sheep from goats"* (Matthew 25:32).

Soon believers will be forced to choose God's way or man's way. This is why our being firmly established in God's Word is so important. We must have faith and confidence in His Word. Remember, His Word is Him, it is so powerful. All truth is contained in His Words, everything is contained in His Words, from His Creation, to His covenants, to his promises.

We are living in the time of the preparation of the church, and what a time to be alive in Him! The strength of our trust is the foundation of our faith. You cannot build without a firm foundation, especially your cornerstone. It is impossible to build anything without a firm foundation. You must have complete faith and trust in His Word and what is His Word, but Him!

The most common theme of Abba's love in the Old Covenant is He being the provider for His people and subsequently Him demanding they follow His ways. If not there is a consequence in that disobedience. Page after page, God is telling us, reminding His children of who He is, what He has done, what He will do either for their good or for their punishment if there is disobedience on their part.

In Psalms 18, David is telling us God is his (our) deliverer. David did not leave his God, abandon his God, he trusted his God. This is why God honored Him, was merciful to him, and delivered him from his enemies. I encourage you to read this Psalm in its entirety. It is, for me, a very wonderful description of our Abba's love and care over us, truly one of my favorite Psalms.

David acknowledges "**It is all about God**," 100% about Him, completely about Abba. This is something we must understand and it must permeate every cell of our being. We are nothing, we are lost, and we are adrift without our God. God gave us David as an example. He was a sinful man, but when confronted with his sin he truly repented. He turned away from his sin and turned to his God for forgiveness. David truly understood and had faith and trust in Abba as a forgiving God. He knew Him as the God of redemption! A part of the act of repentance, what we often overlook, is the fact that "God is faithful to **forgive** and **FORGET**." David had that faith, that confidence, that understanding that God is just that, faithful to forgive and forget!

How often do we say things in reference to our walk with God that is not scriptural? We actually remind God of our sinful past and even question our own salvation. This is very tough to hear, but what you are really saying is, "Yeshua, your death was not sufficient, your Word is not true." I thank God He is so understanding of our failings when we doubt Him. If Abba says our sins are forgiven and forgotten... **THEY ARE FORGIVEN AND FORGOTTEN!!!!!** Why do we feel the need to live in the past? To remain in and wallow in this? The accuser would love for us to live in the past as a defeated body.

Psalms 103:12 says

[12] "*He has removed our sins from us as far as the east is from the west*".

As all of you mathematicians will recognize, this is infinity. That's pretty wide, pretty extreme, a lot of love in that one simple scripture. A'ha'va, unconditional love. David was forever after God's heart.

Abba, again, we pray for Your Light to shine truth into darkness. Father, will you show us a glimpse of Your Heart in all of this, Your Word.

CHAPTER 17

We Must See Life Through Messiah's Eyes, For We are Myopic (Near Sighted) We Need His Corrective Lenses

---∝---

We experience life through our perspective, through our eyes, through our experiences, which are typically flawed. We must experience life through God's perspective. He sees the big picture, He sees the past, the present, and the future. We typically see the present, forget the past, and ignore the future. We look in the mirror, walk away, and forget what we look like. Joseph's life is such an example of this. We all know the story, but Joseph lived the story and truly very few men who have lived could have lived his story without some anger or bitterness.

Your brothers hate you and decide to kill you. Instead, they sell you as a slave and you end up in Egypt (bondage) wrongfully accused of a crime you did not commit. Then, ultimately, you end up as the number two man in all of the land and the savior of your family that hated you, tried to kill you, and sold you as a slave. And I complain about my life??? Really??

Joseph's life is THE example of Romans 8:28, and yet, never did Joseph rebel against his Abba. There seemed to be this understanding that God was in control and that he could trust and believe his God through all circumstances, no matter how dire they may be. Our life is the evidence of our faith.

Father Abba, may our life be a pleasing fragrance to you, lived out for you and by you as we yield control to you.

Chapter 18

Abba Does Not Need Our Help, Just Our Hearts

---⊂✗⊃---

God's Word is complete. It does not require man's additional opinions, ideas, theories, etc. He tells us to follow Him and we must remember, He is His **Word**.

[19] "Yeshua said unto them, 'Come after me, and I will make you fishers for men!'
[20] At once they left their nets and went with Him" (Matthew 4:19-20).
[34] "Then Yeshua called the crowd and His talmidim (disciples) to Him and told them, 'If anyone wants to come after me, let him say 'no' to himself, and take up his execution- stake, and keep following Me.

> ³⁵ *For whoever wants to save his own life will destroy it, but whoever destroys his life for my sake and for the sake of the Good News will save it.*
> ³⁶ *Indeed, what will it benefit a person if he gains the whole world but forfeits his life?*
> ³⁷ *What could a person give in exchange for his life?*
> ³⁸ *For if someone is ashamed of me **and of what I say** in this adulterous and sinful generation, the Son of Man also will be ashamed of him when He comes in His Father's glory with the holy angels'"* (Mark 8:34-38).

Abba woke me up this morning at 0400 and once again reiterated how understanding the precepts of His Word, how it is complete, it is truth, it is life, it is the foundation to knowing who He is. His Word says it is Him, therefore, if it is Him, there can be no darkness, no lies, no deception, and no half-truths. This understanding and belief is foundational for His Church. If I sit in the garage, it does not make me a car. If I sit in church, it does not make me a believer. What differentiates us, is our **TRUST!!**

Yeshua is returning to and for His Bride, His Church. He is not returning to prepare her, He is returning for her. The sooner we get ready, the sooner Messiah returns! Now doesn't that sound great? No more war, hatred, murder, rape, crime. Come soon, but we mustn't be selfish. God is not through filling His kingdom.

The desert experience was a pre-preparation of the Bride, the fulfillment of God's plan, not our plan, not man's plan, but His plan. Even Moses reminded God of this.

^{25} *"So I fell down before Adonai for forty days and nights; I lay there; because Adonai had said He would destroy you.*

^{26} *I prayed to Adonai; I said, 'Adonai! God! Don't destroy your people, your inheritance! You redeemed them through your greatness, you brought them out of Egypt with a strong hand!*

^{27} *Remember your servants Avraham, Yitz'chak and Ya'akov! Don't focus on the stubbornness of this people, or on their wickedness or on their sin.*

^{28} *Otherwise, the land you brought us out of will say, it is because Adonai wasn't able to bring them into the land He promised them and because He hated them that He brought them out to kill them in the desert.*

29 But in fact they are Your people, Your inheritance, whom You brought out by your great power and Your outstretched arm'" (Deuteronomy 9:25-29).

We read how God was angry with Israel and told Moses He was going to destroy them all and make a new covenant with Moses and his family, but Moses' heart was so pure he pled with God and reminded God of His promise, His original covenant with His children. Wow!! Our hearts need to be like Moses'.

We talk about good hearts, a good Godly person, Moses is definitely one of the best to me. He cried and pled with God to keep His covenant with the Hebrew children, rather than stroke his own ego and be God's new covenant. Wow! That is a selfless man of God, no ego there.

For one solid month, 31 days, God told me twice a day every day, "It's all about Me." Now as I was reading, I did in fact notice that it was very difficult to go just one page without reading something about Yahweh's nature, something He did for His people, something He created, an act of His, something He made, caused, etc. It truly is about His heart towards His people, His love and care and concern over us! **It truly is all about Him!!**

Through the desert experience we must recognize God's promises are true, righteous and just. This includes His promises of destruction, not just the good. When the church comes to the place where we accept our role in God's plan we will be fulfilling His plan and be a church prepared. We will be ready for His return. It is in our giving into Him and His ways, understanding it is all about Him, all about our allowing Him to live His life through us. It is Him "in" us, that is life in Messiah, being open to his leading.

The accuser tries to infiltrate "every" aspect of our lives with his lies, his counterfeit to God's reality. Some of his deceptions are very obvious, while others are very subtle. Remember, God desires, asks, and demands we walk the "Highway of Holiness," which is His path for us. While Diablo's tries to drag us off the Highway of Holiness to his road that leads to destruction, that leads to a life separated from Abba.

Abba, Our desire is to walk Your Highway of Holiness and not veer to the right or to the left, but to follow You always. Show us Your way and teach us to love Your creation.

Chapter 19

We Must Learn to Recognize the accusers Subtleties, For They Are Bondage to Us

---∝---

Much of the Church is in bondage and must shed, must be freed from these chains to move on in the Lord. Only God offers true freedom, any other "freedom" outside of His Word isn't freedom, but is bondage! Recognizing these subtle differences is key to a fulfilled, victorious life versus a life in bondage to the accuser. Please understand, we can be in bondage, but it is not necessarily an issue of salvation, not a Heaven or hell issue, more an issue of trust, of pleasing God.

[5] *"The P'rusim (Pharisees) and the Torah-teachers (Law) asked Him, 'Why don't your talmidim*

(disciples) live in accordance with the Tradition of the Elders, but instead eat with ritually unclean hands?'

⁶ Yeshua answered them, 'Yesha'yahu (Isaiah) was right when he prophesied about you hypocrites-as it is written,' 'These people honor me with their lips, But their hearts are far away from me.

⁷ Their worship of me is useless, because they teach man-made rules as if they were doctrines'.

⁸ You depart from God's command and hold unto human tradition.

⁹ 'Indeed,' he said to them, 'You have made a fine art of departing from God's command in order to keep your tradition!'" (Mark 7:5-9).

As a believer our desire should always be to **please** God, to want to do His will, to be found working for Him, living a life of **trust** in Him. When we strike out on our own, in our own strength, our thoughts, our ideas that go against His Word, the results will be ours and not His. Abba, truly has a perfect plan that *"Is in Heaven"* and when followed, will bring the best results and the best fruit. This should always be our desire, to follow Him in His ways, not follow man and his thoughts, his ways.

Should we celebrate Christian holidays or Yahweh's Holy Days? For they are His Days. Should the congregation sing and praise God, or the worship team only? This may seem trivial, but I do not believe it is. Do we eat the food our God made and said we could eat, or do we listen to the accuser and avoid foods God said are "good?" When we follow the path the enemy has placed before us, rather than following God, we are in bondage.

We can illustrate in these three examples the truth of this being bondage. We know for a fact that Yahweh ordained the Holy Days and in doing so included the Goy (gentile) and they were a forever, a perpetual ordinance or statute. We know God made all food and told us what we can eat. We know that God loves our worship and praise for Him.

*[14] "This will be a day for you to remember and celebrate as a festival to Adonai from generation to generation you are to celebrate it by a **perpetual regulation**"* (Exodus 12:14).

[19] "During those seven days, no leaven is to be found in your houses. Whoever eats food with hametz (leaven) in it is to be cut off from the community of

Isra'el- it doesn't matter whether he is a **foreigner or a citizen of the land**" (Exodus 12:19).

⁴² "This was a night when Adonai kept vigil to bring them out of the land of Egypt, and this same night continues to be a night when **Adonai keeps vigil for all of the people of Isra'el through all their generations**" (Exodus 12:42).

¹⁴ "If a **foreigner** is staying with you and wants to observe Pesach (Passover) for Adonai, he is to do it according to the regulations and rules of Pesach- you are to have the same law for the foreigner as for the citizen of the land" (Numbers 9:14).

¹⁴ "When the time came, Yeshua and the emissaries (disciples) reclined at the table,

¹⁵ and He said to them, '**I have really so much wanted to celebrate this Seder with you before I die!**

¹⁶ For I tell you, it is certain that **I will not celebrate it again until it is given its full meaning in the Kingdom of God**'" (Luke 22:14-16).

Wow! How often do we overlook Messiah Yeshua's own Words in reference to celebrating the Passover with us in the millennial reign/Heaven. Most of us were taught that He was referring to the communion service, but that just is not correct. All of you English Majors see that in two connected sentences; Messiah Yeshua is telling His disciples *"I have really **wanted so much** to celebrate **this Seder** with you before I die."* He is not done there. In His next breath He says *"For I tell you, **it is certain** that I will not **celebrate it*** (the Seder) ***again until** it is given its full meaning in the Kingdom of God."* These are not my words, it is not my interpretation, it is our Messiah's Words, it is His heart speaking. He then performs the blessing over the wine and the bread, which is a part of the Seder and that becomes the "communion" we now do, but it did not replace the Passover Seder. The Seder is far more than communion alone.

So we have Yahweh telling us the Passover is a perpetual Ordinance; telling us it is, to this day, a special night where He keeps vigil over His people. Messiah Yeshua telling us He will do it again and the Church leaders today telling us, "That is not for us today, we have something better." We know the early Church celebrated the Pesach (Passover), in fact they celebrated all of the Holy Days, Purim, and the Festival of Lights. We know this because we can read it in the bible. Jesus Himself was in the temple for the "Festival of Sukkot (tents) and the Festival of lights (Hanukkah)."

⁸ *"You, go up to the festival; as for me, I am not going up to this festival now, because the right time for me has not yet come.'*
⁹ *Having said this, he stayed on in the Galil (Galilee).*
¹⁰ *But after His brothers had gone up to the festival, He too went up, not publicly but in secret"* (John 7:8-10).
²² *"Then came Hanukkah in Yerushalayim (Jerusalem). It was winter,*
²³ *and Yeshua was walking inside the Temple area, in Shlomo's (Solomon's) Colonnade"* (John 10:22-23).

Somewhere along the way the Church decided to do away with the Holy Days and institute pagan holidays as days for us to remember our Messiah. Think of it this way, when you have to defend what the bible says versus what man says, there is a big disconnect and I personally do not want to be in that position. God requires no defense and does not require apologies. His word is truth and Life!

We Must Recognize the accusers Subtleties

Why do we need to celebrate easter? It is named after the pagan goddess Astarte, or Estra, the goddess of fertility who is worshipped around the world with colorful eggs. Does this sound familiar to you? How and why we celebrate Yeshua's resurrection, with an easter egg hunt, I'll never understand. We cannot believe that God is *pleased* with our replacement for His most Holy of Holy Days. Remember Exodus 12:42, Yahweh, **still *(to this day)* honors** His people on this night. You must also remember that we are His people. I want His special protection that night. I want **EVERYTHING** Abba has to offer me.

Our actions tell Him, "we have something better than what you gave us!" We should, as a body, celebrate Messiah Yeshua's resurrection, absolutely, but it should be God's way, not man's way. Jesus tells us He will celebrate the Passover Seder with us again! Isn't that exciting?! Doesn't that speak to your heart about who He is? What is important to Him?

The story of Hizkiyahu (Hezekiah) is a great illustration of this. His father, King Achaz (Ahaz) did not do what was right from the perspective of Adonai.

¹"Achaz was twenty years old when he began his reign, and he ruled sixteen years in Yerushalayim. But he did not do what was right from the perspective of Adonai, as David his ancestor had done. ² Rather, he lived in the manner of the kings of Isra'el and made cast metal images for the ba'alim" (2 Chronicles 28:1-2). Hizkiyahu on the other hand did was right in the sight of Yahweh.

³"In the first month of the first year of his reign, he reopened the doors of the house of Adonai and repaired them.

⁴ Then he brought in the cohanim (priests) and L'vi'im (Levites), assembled them in the open space to the east,

⁵ and said to them, 'Listen to me, L'vi'im: consecrate yourselves now, consecrate the house of Adonai the God of your ancestors and remove the filth from the Holy Place'" (2 Chronicles 29:3-5).

Why is this story significant? Ahaz followed the pagan ways of the people in the neighboring kingdoms and towns and abandoned the God of Israel. Paganism in any form has **NO PLACE IN THE BODY OF MESSIAH!!** If something was pagan to the ancient of days it is pagan today! It does not become less pagan over time. Is the accuser less evil over time? God has given us many examples in His word in reference to this problem, beginning in the desert. If you follow the story of Hezekiah you will see that after cleansing the Temple and rededicating it, the first holy day they celebrated was Pesach (Passover).

¹ "Then Hizkiyahu sent to all Isra'el and Y'hudah, and wrote letters also to Efrayim (Ephraim) and M'nasheh (Manasses), summoning them to the house of Adonai in Yerushalayim, to keep the Pesach to Adonai the God of Isra'el.
² For the king, his officials and the entire Yerushalayim community had agreed to keep the Pesach in the second month.
³ They had not been able to observe it at the proper time because the cohanim had not consecrated themselves in sufficient number; also the people had not assembled in Yerushalayim.
⁴ The idea had seemed right to the king and to the whole community;
⁵ so they issued a decree that it should be proclaimed throughout all Isra'el, from Be'er-Sheva (Beer-Sheva) to Dan, that they should come to

keep the Pesach to Adonai the God of Isra'el at Yerushalayim; for only a few had been observing it as prescribed" (2 Chronicles 30:1-5).

This scripture truly parallels what has happened and is happening in the church today. The church stopped celebrating Passover, but a few understand the connection and are beginning to do so. Yeshua will bring it back.

Once again, this may seem trivial, but corporate praise is so very important to the body, for **God inhabits and loves the praises of His people!** I live in the north suburbs of Detroit and have attended numerous churches looking for a home church. Many of the churches have a time of worship, but it is the worship team on stage singing as the congregation sits and listens. God wants worshippers, not just a select few. When I vacation in Florida I will attend church there also. There I experienced the worship team leader singing songs that were actually difficult for him, while the people stood and just listened. Understand, I am not talking a song or two, I am talking the entire worship service.

That is not corporate worship, it is someone stroking their own ego. The whole Idea behind the worship team is to lead the people in worship, not a display for their talents or egos. His Word says in Psalms 22:3

³ *"Nevertheless, you are Holy, enthroned on the praises of Isra'el."* Abba desires our praises, for He inhabits them.

⁸ *"Each of the four living beings had six wings and was covered with eyes inside and out; and **day** and **night** they **never stop saying,***

'Holy, holy, holy is Adonai, God of Heaven's armies the one who was, who is and who is coming!'

⁹ *And whenever the living beings give glory, honor and thanks to the One sitting on the throne, to the One who lives forever and ever,*

¹⁰ *the 24 elders fall down before the One sitting on the throne, who lives forever and ever, and worship Him. They throw their crowns in front of the throne and say,*

'You are worthy, Adonai Eloheinu (Lord our God), to have glory, honor and power,
Because you created all things-

*Yes, because of your will they were created
And came into being!'"* (Revelations 4:8-10).

There are times while praising Abba, I find myself lost in Him, I am in His pocket.

When we ignore God's Word we are in err and are in bondage to the enemy. If it is our ego doing something, it is not God. There is no neutrality in God, we are either with Him or the accuser. You must understand there is not a third choice. I cannot say that enough!!

[11] *"God said, 'Let the earth put forth grass, seed-producing plants, and fruit trees, each yielding its own kind of seed-bearing fruit, on the earth'; and that is how it was.*

[12] *The earth brought forth grass, plants each yielding its own kind of seed, and trees each producing its own kind of seed-bearing fruit;* **and God saw that it was good**" (Genesis 1:11-12).

[20] *"God said, 'Let the water swarm with swarms of living creatures, and let birds fly above the earth in the open dome of the sky.'*

[21] *God created the great sea creatures and every living thing that creeps, so that the water swarmed*

with all kinds of them, and there was every kind of winged bird; **and God saw that it was good**" (Genesis 1:20-21).

[24] "God said, 'Let the earth bring forth each kind of living creature-each kind of livestock, crawling animal and wild beast'; and that is how it was.

[25] God made each kind of wild beast, each kind of livestock and every kind of animal that crawls along the ground; **and God saw that it was good**" (Genesis 1:24-25).

[29] "Then God said, 'Here! Throughout the whole earth I am giving you as food every seed-bearing plant and every tree with seed bearing fruit'" (Genesis 1:29).

[3] "Every moving thing that lives will be food for you; just as I gave you green plants before, so now I give you everything-

[4] only flesh with its life, which is its blood, you are not to eat" (Genesis 9:3-4).

In these scriptures we have God telling us that He created our fruits, our veggies and our meats. Please notice the last 7 words of each of these creations: **"and God saw that it was good."** God is telling us what he created is **good,** this truly requires no explanation. In Genesis 9:4, God is telling Noah and his family what they may eat, which pretty much includes everything. In Romans we are told if we are eating in doubt, and not on trust, we are in sin.

²³ "But the doubter comes under condemnation if he eats, because his action is not based on trust. And anything not based on trust is sin" (Romans 14:23).

We now as believers have a decision to make: Do we "trust" God's Word and eat what He has created and told us we may eat? Or do we listen to the accuser and avoid these foods God has said are good? To answer the question or the arguments regarding GMO and organic, you must understand and trust the simple fact that God truly knew the future of food, the path it would take at the hands of man. When we follow man in this regard, we are telling God, "You had no idea what man was going to do to food, you really had no idea what was to come." It is truly all about **TRUST!!** It is all about trusting Abba's heart towards us and that His Word is **TRUSTWORTHY and TRUE!**

Please understand **ALL** food should be eaten in moderation. I am not supporting overeating. Even water in copious amounts over a short period of time can kill you. God does not say, "Eat as much as you want anytime." Gluttony is bondage. Also, eat a diet that suits you, your lifestyle and body condition.

The three best examples off the top of my head are gluten, lactose, and animal fats (meat). As far as gluten or lactose is concerned, for those who have a problem, the symptoms are real. But where do those symptoms come from? Prior to the fall, sickness/illness/disease was not a part of the garden, they came in after the fall of man. Sickness was introduced at the fall in sin. We must remember, the accuser has counterfeit of what God has made and he wants you to follow him and not God. He wants you walking on his path in **"all"** his counterfeit ways. Any time that he can pull you from God; that is a battle or a skirmish won by him. These are not Heaven or hell issues, just issues of recognizing the enemy and trusting Abba. I know the hearts of God's people are towards our Abba and not the accuser! We just need to be aware of his subtle ways.

[1] *"Now the serpent was more crafty than any wild animal which Adonai, God had made."* (Genesis 3:1).

14 "There is nothing surprising in that, for the adversary himself masquerades as an angel of light" (2 Corinthians 11:14).
7 "Throw all your anxieties upon Him, because He cares about you.
8 Stay sober, stay alert! Your enemy the adversary stalks about like a roaring lion looking for someone to devour" (1 Peter 5:7-8).

We see here in these scriptures a description of the accuser as a very subtle and crafty one who will get you when you are unaware. Understand, when you read 1 Peter 5: 7-8, it does not say *"stalks about as a..."*, but, *"**like a** roaring lion."* The difference is this: the hunting lion is very stealthy, and he is not roaring, but he is vicious in his hunting like a loud scary roaring lion! If the accuser approached you as the devil, you would never accept his offerings. He is subtle, crafty, he comes as an angel of light. This is why we are told to, *"Stay sober, stay alert!!"*

Your Bride's desire is that You open our eyes, unstop our ears, and soften our hearts to you Abba. Oh father, show us Your glory and teach us your ways. Restore your Church in the name of our Messiah Yeshua, Amen

Chapter 20

Warnings to the Churches III

———⚯———

Let us look at God's word in reverse by starting in Revelations. In the first few chapters of Revelations we find warnings to the seven churches, not warnings to the world, but very specifically to the churches. We all know and understand this, but I believe we all too often look at this and point our fingers at others not understanding we are in one of, some of, or most of these churches!

These can be both the body and individuals. They are spiritual states, so one can be a member of more than one of these spiritual states. What are described are people still in the desert and not following God, His Word. They are in bondage to the enemy. In July of 2015, God gave me a vision where

I was with Him in the Heavens looking down upon the Earth and something began to float from the Earth into Heaven. It started with a few and within 3 seconds my view of the earth was obscured. As they floated upwards I could then distinguish they were chains floating into the heavens. He told me, "It was the church being set free from its bondage to the accuser."

Understand, we are in bondage to satan when we take the path satan has given us and do not follow the path God has for us. The Highway of Holiness is God's path, "anything" else is bondage. That is **"ANYTHING"** else. We can make excuses for our choices, but if it is not of God (His Word), it is of satan. This is one of those "let it sink in moments." Every time, not sometime, not every other time, not a once in a while time, but every time we choose a path not of our God, we are choosing the path of the enemy. We are saying, "no God, the accuser has something better, his counterfeit is better than Your plan, better than the original." Truly, please stop here and think about that. If you find yourself defending man's word over God's word, you are not in the best of positions. Please understand this does not please God. "Many who are first, will be last"

You must understand, the accuser has a counterfeit for virtually every single thing God made or that man, through his creativity, has come up with. There are truly so many examples, literally too many to mention. To explain this as simply as I possibly can, Abba created sex, the accuser created porn; God created food, the accuser created gluttony; God made the family, the accuser created homosexuality; man created the computer for man's good and the accuser uses it to rob, steal and destroy lives. Seriously, you right now are probably thinking of 100 things that I have not thought. Remember, in whatever we do, we are either serving God or the enemy. A very disturbing and unfortunate truth is that the accuser has counterfeit believers and churches (remember the warnings in Revelations).

God in his word, has promises for us which are directly related to our behavior, to the decisions we make. Reread the old covenant looking at God's Word with this precept in mind. He never tells us to take a day off from following His Word, from listening to His voice, from obeying His Commands. Abba's Word says, the law of the Lord is good. Please understand, I am not saying you have to be perfect, we don't and in fact, we cannot be, at least not now.

Let me introduce you to my Abba

We just have to have a heart that is always earnestly seeking our Abba, always turning and returning to Him. That really is the believer's life, a life of turning towards the Light, seeking after Him.

Abba, Open our eyes to you, help us to recognize the accuser and his ways. It is our desire to be found following you, your ways, not to be walking in the ways of the accuser.

Chapter 21

All of Yahweh's Promises are Ours, Including His Punishments

---∝---

As previously mentioned, prior to the ministry of Yeshua, we had the written law to determine what behaviors and actions God deemed sinful and required atonement by a sacrifice. These sins were things we physically did, things of actions. He changed the laws to sins of the heart, a mere thought was considered to be the same as actual sin. No longer did you have to steal to be in sin, but now if you were coveting, you were in sin. God in His goodness and Mercy understood the difficulty we would face in trying to live this life expected of us, and He sent the Holy Spirit as our comforter and guide.

Look at Peter's actions before and after. Actually, look at the disciples before and after. Two complete and total opposites. The Holy Spirit gives us a conscience and a boldness we otherwise would not have. He helps us in living out the life we are called to live, but only by His presence in our lives every moment of every day can we do so. We are so incredibly blessed to have Him living in us, if we follow Him, for it takes more than just hearing Him. All of this being said, we must remember God is a just God and the unrepentant heart awaits punishment,

⁵ "Since you already know all this, my purpose is only to remind you that Adonai, who once delivered the people from Egypt, later destroyed those who did not trust.

⁶ And the angels that did not keep within their original authority, but abandoned their proper sphere, He has kept in darkness, bound with everlasting chains for the Judgment of the Great Day.

⁷ And S'dom (Sodom), 'Amora (Gomorrah) and the surrounding cities, following a pattern like theirs, committing sexual sins and perversions , lie exposed

as a warning of the everlasting fire awaiting those who must undergo punishment" (Jude 1:5-7).

So there are questions we should ask ourselves today: How are we doing in following His guidance? Do we always recognize His voice? Do we see some of our difficulties as His promise of punishment for our disobedience to His Word? Do we do things that are displeasing to God? Do we always call on Him in times of trouble? Do we follow His Word exclusively? Or do we keep one foot in and one out? Do we even recognize we are doing This? Do we understand the consequences of our actions? Do we understand that our actions are words to Abba?

Yahweh's Words are action— He speaks and it happens!! Our actions are our words, for our actions come from our hearts. Our words and actions do not always line up. We say things to Abba in our actions, in our trust or in our lack of trust!

We mustn't confuse Yahweh's chastisement as abandonment. When He chastises you, is He abandoning you? His Word tells us it is out of His love, out of care and concern that He does this, to bring us back to Him. Remember, as a Gentile believer in God, as a follower of God, you are adopted and grafted into the Jewish family. **You are now a part of Abba's Jewish family!!** This thought, this truth should not be cause for any negativity in your walk with Abba.

² "I will make of you a great nation, I will bless you, and I will make your name great; and you are to be a blessing.

³ I will bless those who bless you, but I will curse anyone who curses you; **and by you all the families of the earth will be blessed**" (Genesis 12:2-3). This scripture tells us how Abba feels about His people, how much He cares for them, for us.

Everything of God, about God, yesterday, today and forever goes back to the Garden, goes back to His original plan. It all began there: "In the beginning, God created……" Abba's plan for man, for man's future, for his life, began in the Garden called Eden and ends in the ultimate Gan-Eden (pleasure). It started with perfection and will end in perfection. Sin made its way into the Garden and Earth, so it must be destroyed and rebuilt. Our Abba cannot be physically with sin. We can read Yeshua's last words,

³⁴ *"Elohi! Elohi! L'mah sh'vaktani? (Which means, **"My God! My God! Why have you deserted me?"**)* (Mark 15:34).

Now read John 16:32:

³² *"But a time is coming–indeed it has come already–when you will be scattered, each one looking out for himself; and **you will leave me all alone. Yet I am not alone; because the Father is with me"***.

I think we gloss over his last word too quickly; Messiah Yeshua the Son of God was absolutely confident Abba would never forsake him, never leave Him, yet He did. Yeshua had to go this last step on His own. When it did happen, he was shocked. His last words were not trite, simple, meaningless words, but words from his heart. God cannot be with sin. He lived with the Hebrew children in the Holy of Holies.

This brings us to the "true church." It starts, where else, but in Genesis, in Gan-Eden. We already discussed this was Abba's original intent, to have fellowship with His creation, walking with, talking with, sharing with, enjoying His people. Once again it started this way, went off course, but it will end this way. The church must find its way back to the Garden.

We must go back to our roots to fully comprehend the analogy of the bride, the groom, the wedding, and the Jewish roots of all of this. It, the ancient Jewish wedding, I believe, parallels the actual events to take place in the end. The groom making his intents known to the bride, then waiting for the bride to prepare herself and the eventual marriage. For us the groom is waiting for our preparation and when we ready ourselves, He will return! A side note: there are not two marriages, two weddings, one for the Jews and one for the Gentiles, there is but **ONE Bride, ONE Wedding and one flock**!

[16] *"Also I have other sheep which are not from this pen; I need to bring them, and they will hear my voice; and there will one flock, one Shepherd"* (John 10:16).

Let's talk about Replacement Theology, which is based upon nothing more than Anti-Semitism. Nowhere in God's word does He ever completely cut off His chosen people. Abba always has a remnant of followers. It is through these faithful people that He displays His faithfulness. There were and are many, many times where He was angry and upset with them, but never has He or did He end His covenant with the Jews. Abba dispersed (the Diaspora) them into other countries, often times under bondage. But He always, after a time, rescues them and ultimately brought them back to Eretz Yisrael and to Himself in fulfillment of His covenant. He is THE God of forever. He is THE God of promise, of faithfulness to His covenant. It is we, the sheep, who go astray not our Abba. It is never Him who changes, it is always us.

Anti-Semitism is rooted in sin. If we just look at history and the people who have tried to annihilate the Jewish people, it is very evident these were evil people. Haman and Hitler come to mind immediately. These men tried to **completely** eliminate the Jewish people. Today we have many Muslim leaders who espouse this same anti-Semitic rhetoric. In this rhetoric they include *"All Believers,"* God's people!

Abba, this is your design, your plan, your heart. Open our eyes, ears and hearts to You Abba, to Your will. Our desire is your best for us Father. In the name of Your son Yeshua, Amen

CHAPTER 22

Our First Love

———⋈———

Revelations is our preparation manual, our go by if you will, especially for the day we live in. In Revelations 2: 1-7, we read of the warning to the Messianic community in Ephesus. This is the first warning to any of the Messianic communities. Please remember, **OUR ABBA DOES NOT DO ANYTHING IN A VACUUM, EVERYTHING HE DOES HAS A REASON, EVERYTHING HAS A PURPOSE, EVERYTHING IS ABOUT HIS PLAN,** for our Abba does have a plan, a **perfect plan** for you and for me.

[1] "To the angel of the Messianic community in Ephesus, write: Here is the Message from the one

who holds the seven stars in His right hand and walks among the seven gold menorahs:

² I know what you have been doing how hard you have worked, how you have persevered, and how you can't stand wicked people; so you tested those who call themselves emissaries but aren't– you found them to be liars.

³ You are persevering and you have suffered for my sake without growing weary.

⁴ But I have this against you: you lost the love you had at first.

⁵ Therefore, remember where you were before you fell and turn from this sin and do what you used to do before. Otherwise, I will come to you and remove your menorah from its place–if you don't turn from your sin!

⁶ But you have this in your favor: you hate what the Nicolaitians do–I hate it too.

⁷ Those who have ears, let them hear what the Spirit is saying to the Messianic communities. To him winning the victory I will the right to eat from the Tree of Life which is in God's Gan–Eden" (Revelation 2:1-7).

So what was their first love? If we look in Jeremiah 2:2, we can read about this first love:

² *"I remember your devotion when you were young; how, as a bride, **you loved me; how you followed me through the desert, through a land not sown.**"*

I really do not have to tell you Abba was your first love, but we must look at how He describes that first love, this is very important. Remember, Abba **never** makes us guess as to what He expects from us. He describes our first love literally in one small sentence, one seemingly innocuous sentence: *"**how you followed me through the desert, through a land not sown.**"*

I also do not have to tell you the desert is your life in Him, **ALL** of your experiences in life leading up to the end. But what does it mean? To keep it very simple, it is all about trusting Him, trusting our Abba, being confident in trusting He will take care of me, trusting that He loves me every moment of everyday, trusting He is who He says He is, and trusting He has a plan for **ME**!!

Our First Love

We must go back to the exodus from Egypt or, on a more personal note, our exodus from bondage, from our sin filled life. Can you imagine someone approaching you today and asking you to physically just walk away from your home and oh, by the way, we are going to take a walk in the desert, a land not sown. Believe me the Hebrew people knew about the desert, it surrounded them, they lived in it, and they toiled in it. If you have never flown into Cairo, Egypt, it is a visual experience like no other. It is brown everywhere except a few green golf courses. It truly is a sight to behold with sand blowing across the roads and piling up, shutting down portions of the road.

Abba chose the community of Ephesus first and I believe the reason was to go back to the beginning, our first encounter with Abba, which began in Gan–Eden, the Garden. For the Garden was His original plan for man, and everything goes back to Gan-Eden. This is where relationship began, and this is where sin and bondage began, in the Garden. It is His heart to lead us out of bondage by following Him, not by following man, not by figuring things out for ourselves, but by trusting in and following Him, our Dear Father, our Abba.

Let me introduce you to my Abba

⁷ "To him winning the victory I will the right to eat from the Tree of Life which is in God's Gan–Eden" (Revelations 2:7).

Their first love was a love of and a complete trust in Abba. It had to be, otherwise you would never leave the confines of your home to follow Abba through the desert. It is all about trust, but that trust is in Him and His Word, for His Word is Him. Going back to the desert story: this love story, Abba gave His people His Laws, His Word, He gave them the Sabbath, the Holy Days, victories, the sacrificial system, food, water, clothing that did not wear out, etc. He gave them everything they needed. My brothers and sisters, wherever in this world you are, it is truly about trusting Him, His Word and not putting your trust in man. It is about trusting Him, who is infallible. Not man, not me, it is about trusting Him, trusting His Word, believing His Word, living His Word. **It is all about Abba!!**

Please understand, I am completely aware and know that Abba uses man often times to provide for our needs, but our trust is still in Him. Allow me to give a personal example. In February 2016 I had surgery. The surgeon made his plans of how the procedure would go, he even drew me a picture. I had confidence in his abilities and I trusted him to do his best. But, I also prayed to Abba and asked Him to speak to the surgeon when he got inside ready to do the surgery. My prayer was that he would hear God and do what God was telling him to do. I have no idea of my surgeon's belief in God, but that really was not relevant, for I had complete confidence that my God knew precisely what needed to be done and knew how to convey this to him. I am happy and blessed to report that is precisely what happened. Once inside, he changed his mind as to how to perform the procedure, and in this decision any possible complications were avoided. Recovery was much quicker and easier! Our God is faithful!!

Father, Take us back to our first love, and show us the way and guide us back to you.

Chapter 23

Warnings to the Churches IV

―――――∝―――――

If you read the warnings in Revelations and think of someone else, another denomination, or person, or people, you are on very shaky ground. These are warnings to "**EVERY MEMBER**" of the body of Messiah, "**everyone**" in the church, to all of us believers, hence, the warning to the churches. You should never just assume you are of Smyrna or Philadelphia. We need to search our hearts and ask Abba: What in my life is displeasing to you Father, what must I change to be **FULLY and COMPLETELY** pleasing to you? If you cannot see this, stop reading, put this book aside, get down on your face and search your heart in earnest, for the truth. He loves you and will reveal to you exactly what He wants, He will show you your preparation work required. That is His heart, He loves us so much. Think of David.

Understand not everything we do is a heaven or hell issue. It is a pleasing God issue, and yet some things are Heaven or hell issues. Matthew 7:21-23 makes it clear we must search our hearts:

[21] *"Not everyone who says to me, 'Lord, Lord!' will enter the Kingdom of Heaven, only those who do what my Father in heaven wants.*
[22] On that Day, many will say to me 'Lord, Lord! Didn't we prophesy in your name? Didn't we expel demons in your name? Didn't we perform miracles in your name?'
[23] Then I will tell them to their faces, 'I never knew you! **Get away from me, you workers of lawlessness!***"*

This passage sounds to me to be very much like a heaven or hell issue. The word "**lawlessness**" means to transgress the law and that law is God's law, it certainly is not man's law. This scripture should cause us to drop to our knees and seek Abba's face, even if we feel we are not transgressing

His law, we should be open to the Holy Spirit's guidance and He will reveal any transgressions on our part, for we are sometimes not aware.

So our prayer should be, "Abba, which of Your laws have I transgressed or am I transgressing? What of my life is not pleasing to you? Father, it is my desire to offer my life as a living sacrifice to you. Please forgive me and create in me a clean heart and renew a right Spirit in me." Do understand, Abba desires our complete trust in Him. Some of our misgivings are just not pleasing to God. He still loves us, but His plan for us is that full complete walk and trust in Him.

It is His desire we prepare for Him, that we become His bride, and that we have this spiritual intimacy with Him. He loves you so much that He gave His one and only begotten son, our Messiah, our Savior, for **YOU,** to draw **YOU** to Him. Can you see this, this love, this devotion for **YOU**, how truly special Abba thinks **YOU** are? To do this for **YOU**, truly, how very much He loves **YOU**!! Did you catch and Understand this? God desires and wants deeply to have fellowship with **YOU**!! He created **YOU**, He knows **YOU** and He cares about **YOU**. So, in order to have this relationship with **YOU**, He sacrificed His only Son. Now let that sink in. God, Yahweh, Abba, the Creator of the universe loves and cares for **YOU PERSONALLY!!!**

Think about this, we as His children, do not have any prerequisites to have a relationship with Him, but He does have them for us. Abba came to man in the Garden, man did not go to Him. In order for God to have fellowship with us, we must be pure and holy. His desire to have a relationship and fellowship with us ended with Him sending His only begotten Son to die for us, which made a way for us to become holy and enabled us to approach Him!! More significantly, it made a way for Him to come live in us!! His love and desire for **YOU** is on a very real and very deep personal level! Wow!! Did you catch all those **you(s)**? Can you see love in His plan?

These are the Words He speaks over you, Words of blessing and not cursing when we have correct relationship with Him. You have to see how much Abba cares about you, how deep His love goes, How his love for you transcends everything we know and understand.

Understanding, accepting, and getting serious about the warnings in Revelations is the beginning of the return of the church to its original roots, the original intentions God had for us. God often refers to our relationship to Him or with Him to a walk, a walk on a path. There are but two paths we walk, either a path toward God, or the accuser. There is not a third path. Nowhere in the Bible does God refer to a third path. Only the two, one to destruction with the accuser, or one to eternal life with Abba.

The gift, and it is a gift, of eternal life with Him begins the moment we confess our sins and accept Messiah as our savior, our atonement for our sins. Yeshua gave His life for us, His death on the cross was complete and atoned for all sinners and is sufficient to cover "**all**" sin. From, as it is called, the little white lie, to the vilest of sins and every sin in between; I am speaking worldly here for we are all filthy to God.

God set up the sacrificial system and it is He who has set up the way to Him. There are no other options. We cannot get to an eternity with Abba without doing it His way. The same way you cannot enter any venue without the proper ticket to the event, you cannot approach the arena, the stadium or the theatre and offer whatever you determine you would like to give as your entry fee. The entry fee is what has been predetermined by the authorities.

Many people feel they can circumvent God's way and do it their way. There is but one way.

⁶ *"Yeshua said, 'I am the way–and the truth and the life; no one comes to the Father except through me'"* (John 14:6).

Abba, Reveal to your children your love, have an encounter with every man woman and child on earth; show them your love, your heart towards them, let them see your love and glory.

My Chapter

———∝———

This chapter is dedicated to me, to remind me, to bolster my belief and faith in my Abba and His timing, His way, not mine. The best way to say this is, it is truly, always and forever about Him, His timing, and His way in my life in **all** things. I believe God made me a social communal person, beginning with the family. After all, that is where it all began, in the Garden, as was already stated, everything goes back to the Garden.

    I am not a lone wolf, never someone who must have solitude. I do not require alone time, though on rare occasion it is nice to be alone with Abba. I prefer shared time, together time. When we put all this together, God made us a communal social people. He instilled in us that deep desire for fellowship with

Him, with others, with our spouse, with our children, with His creation, with like-minded people.

I am completely aware and cognizant of the fact that we always have our Abba, for He is always with us. I am not saying that He isn't enough, for He is. But that deep desire to share "all" that life has to give, that it has to offer, with that one person on Earth that you live for, is there with you not by chance, but by our Heavenly Father. Placed there by Him, there is synergism in this. I believe we do have a soul mate that fits our DNA, which fits like a glove and is that one person that God has chosen for us. In having said all of this, we still make mistakes: sometimes we miss that person completely due to our own prejudices, desires, rather than listening to God. Sometimes we find the one and then allow the enemy to influence us in our life and we break up. It is never God's plan to cause us pain or sorrow, though he does allow it to happen to us when we stray from Him. Can you imagine (Jer 29:11) how easy His job would be if we just followed His plan? Instead we run interference on His plan and He then has to pick up the pieces and make things right again, though it was not His first choice for us.

We are a microwave society: we want what we want now, not later; we help God rather than wait upon Him. We need to understand that it is not necessary for us to "see the big picture," to know everything going on, it is only necessary we recognize that there is a big picture and that our Abba is absolutely in control.

[8] *"For my thoughts are not your thoughts, and my ways are not your ways, says Adonai"* **(Isaiah 55:8).** All Abba desires are that, "We follow Him through the desert, a land not sown."

Fear has no place in our life, in Abba, only trust. Jeremiah 29:11 is such a powerful scripture if we could just learn to have total trust in Him. The Bible is written to demonstrate to us this trust and until we grasp this truth we are in bondage to the enemy. We must remember there are only two paths we can follow. It is either our Heavenly Father's path or the path of Diablo's. Which path we choose is our decision, being alert to that still small voice is crucial. It is a learning process, learning to recognize and trust the urging of the Holy Spirit, learning to hear and trust His voice.

Father, may our hearts be still and may we know that You are God. May we always recognize your voice and may we choose your path; but when we stray or are in error, may we recognize your voice and come back to you with true repentance and allow you to correct, lead, and guide us.

Chapter 24

Covenant

―――――∝―――――

It is and has always been God's plan to have covenantal relationship with His people. The covenant-maker is the keeper of the covenant, and if over time the covenant is changed, it is the maker who changes it. It is never changed to make it tougher, but it is changed to be more inclusive, made to be more obtainable, than impossible.

The covenant with the Hebrew children was an animal sacrificial system. When Messiah Yeshua came as the Paschal Lamb, He became the final and the ultimate sacrifice for our sins, our atonement allowing us to approach God, to enter the Holy of Holies. A huge aspect of this new covenant was the promise of the Holy Spirit.

Imagine trying to live the believer's life without the Holy Spirit. This is exactly what the Hebrew children faced every day of their lives. We have the promise, the Holy Spirit, and yet we still have difficulty in living, trusting, believing, following our Father. "Oh ye of little faith."

With Abraham, God did not initially make a covenant with him, but gave him instructions which he obeyed. I believe this was very intentional on God's part. He found someone whom He could count on, whom He could trust, who had an unwavering trust and faith in God.

Genesis 15:18-21 holds the first word portion of the covenant dealt with the promise of a land:

[18] *"That day Adonai made a covenant with Avram: 'I have given this land to you and your descendants- from the Vadi (valley) of Egypt to the great river, the Euphrates River-*

[19] *the territory of the Keni (Kenite), the K'nizi (Kenizzite), the Kadmoni (Kadmonites),*

[20] *the Hitti (Hittite), the P'rizi (???), the Refa'im (Rephaim),*

[21] *the Emori (Amorite), the Kena'ani (Canaanite), the Girgashi (Girgashite) and the Yvusi (Jebusite).'"*

This is a whole story unto itself. Remember, God does **nothing** in a vacuum. Eretz Yisrael was physically placed where it remains today, though not all, given to the Hebrews to show God's love, might, and promise to his people, to the world. Many years later God appears to Abraham again and reiterates the covenant speaking first of the people, then the land. God is an orderly God. Circumcision was the sign of this covenant. The Hebrews had a physical land and a physical sign of the covenant, though the land was not in their possession until later, after the enslavement in Egypt. Once again, there is another story there.

We must understand, God did not create the universe, or us, in a vacuum. We and all we see and do not see, have a purpose, a function, and a connection. Understanding, believing and trusting is absolutely key to our faith. God is not the author of confusion. I cringe when I hear believers give credit to the Holy Spirit for something they themselves messed up, something they did wrong, or something they did out of order. This wrong thinking states, in a slightly convoluted way, the Holy Spirit is living in "me and anything I do is because of Him," when proper thinking would be, "I messed up, but the Holy Spirit can take my lemons and make lemonade."

Abba "is not the author of confusion," never has been and never will be to a believer. He can be to a nonbeliever to save the believer.

⁸ "Adonai said to Y'hosuha (Joshua), 'Don't be afraid of them, for I have handed them over to you; not one of their men will stand up against you.'
⁹ Having spent the entire night marching up from Gilgal, Y'ohshua fell upon them, taking them by surprise.
¹⁰ Adonai threw them into confusion before Isra'el and defeated them in a great slaughter at Giv'on (Gibeon), pursuing them along the road that goes up from Beit-Horon (Beth-Horon), and beating them back to Azekah and all the way to Makkedah" (Joshua 10:8-10).

CHAPTER 25

It's Truly all about Trusting Abba, It is Our Foundation

———⊰⊱———

³¹ "So don't be anxious, asking, 'What will we eat? What will we drink? Or How will we be clothed?'
³² For it is the pagans who set their hearts on all these things. Your heavenly Father knows you need them all.
³³ But seek first His Kingdom and His righteousness, and all these things will be given to you as well" (Matthew 6:31-33).

This is truly a law for living the life of the believer. It is a requirement for the mature believer. God's expectation for the grounded believer is to understand this and have faith and trust in Him, in who he says he is, **WHO HE IS!!** He has given us the written Word so we can read and reread the stories of His love for us, His might, His power, His faithfulness towards His people. Remember, God is His word and we can 1,000% trust His Word, for it is Him.

We must discuss our **thoughts** here. It is important that we must understand not all our thoughts are our thoughts. Double talk? No! Let me ask you: Have you ever had a thought and literally asked yourself, "Where did that come from?" It likely was a thought planted by the accuser, placed there for us to take hold of it.

We are told by God in 2 Corinthians 10:5

[5] *"every arrogance that raises itself up against the knowledge of God,* **we take every thought captive and make it obey the Messiah.***"*

A thought in our head is just that, it is in our head. Once we entertain that thought, we take possession of it, we take ownership and it now becomes ours.

In Philippians 4:8 we are told

[8] *"In conclusion brothers, focus your thoughts on what is true, noble, righteous, pure, lovable*

or admirable, on some virtue or on something praiseworthy."

When we do not follow this one very simple passage, we fail in a way so big we cannot imagine. It is a failure of the life the believer is called to. If you look at Philippians it is a very small book, only four chapters, and yet it actually lays out a tenet so vital to the believer's life, his expected actions by God. This is a tenet of how to live our life in God, for He does have expectations in reference to our behavior as followers of Messiah Yeshua.

Read Philippians now and think about what Paul is talking about. It is about the effect our behavior has, the consequences of it. Pay close attention to 1:9-11. Our behavior comes from our thoughts. If we have negative thoughts, we are lacking the love Paul is talking about. There is no overflow of love leading to:

⁹ *"And this is my prayer: that your love may more and more overflow in fullness of knowledge and depth of discernment,*

¹⁰ **so that you will be able to determine what is best and thus be pure and without blame for the day of the Messiah,**

^{11} filled with the fruit of righteousness that comes through Yeshua the Messiah to the glory and praise of God."

Wow! Paul then goes on and uses himself as an example by telling of his situation, of being unjustly put in prison and how some are proclaiming the gospel out of love and others out of jealousy, hoping to cause Him harm.
The result that follows the **"To determine what is best,"** is being, **"pure and without blame for the day of the Messiah."** This day is the day of Messiah's return, it is to His Bride prepared, without spot or wrinkle! In Philippians 1:18, Paul takes these thoughts captive and states

^{18} **"but so what? All that matters is that in every way, whether in honesty or in pretense, the Messiah is being proclaimed and in that I rejoice."**

Can you imagine Paul's situation? Knowing all this and understanding you are likely headed to your death and you always find the good in all things. This should be our life, our cry, our prayer!!!!

Everyone has negative thoughts. We all have negative self-talk. Negative self-talk is a self-enabler. We do not need anybody else to be on our side, to take up our banner because we do it all in our own head. Instead of taking the thought captive, we entertain it and add to it with negative self-talk. Thus, we enable ourselves to depart from Godly behavior. If you think about crimes of any type, negative self-talk is typically involved.

When you hear, "they, she, he deserved it," negative self-talk was/is involved. Just stop and think about this for a moment. If we, as humankind, have nothing but positive, good thoughts about our fellow man, how could there be crime against someone you have no ill will towards? If God were to give me the ability to put one of His tenets into action, it would be Philippians. We could end crime, war, hatred, for negative self-talk is the justification used for the action(s) taken. We just seem to gloss over so much of God's word. We have stopped up ears, blind eyes, and stony hearts.

We do not think like God. Most of the time we look at life through our own perspective and not His. We need to change our thought process, change our perspective. We are no longer "of the earth," we are only "on it."

Father forgive us and teach us to understand what it means to be your Bride prepared. Teach us how you think, what it means to think like You. Take us to where Paul lived in you, his trust, and his peace. Take us to this place. Unstop our ears, open our eyes, and soften our hearts to your words, your truth. May we become your bride prepared.

Chapter 26

One God, One Messiah, One Holy Spirit and One Church

———∝———

In Philippians it talks about the "day of the Messiah." This day is the day of His return to earth (Philippians 1:6). Paul continues in 9-11 and gives a more in-depth account of where our hearts should be upon Messiah's return. Paul describes this by our overflowing love which gives a "fullness of knowledge and depth of discernment," and in this we are able to determine what is **best** in God.

Best connotes there is a good in God, a better in God, and a best in God. Our path we walk in God, the Highway of Holiness, has at its center the best and as we veer off to the right or the left we approach the better, the good, and at some point we are no longer on the Highway of Holiness if we stray too far. At this point we have chosen to give back to God the precious gift of His son's life and resurrection, our salvation. We become the prodigal son. God's best is His word and His word is Him. His plan is His will, not our will, but His, and His will first begins in Heaven and is then put into place here on Earth.

When Yeshua taught His children to pray it was, *"thy will be done on Earth as it is in Heaven."* We must remember and let this sink so very deep within us: it is His idea, His plan, and His will, not ours. It is not we the church taking the things God has given us and changing them, making them better, we deciding to do away with His plan.

Remember Jeremiah 29:11. "I know what plans **I have** for you," again, it is Yahweh's plan. It is all about Him, all about our Abba. He is the giver of life, life forever. We are to follow His ways, not our ways, His design, His plan, for it is truly all about Abba! God makes it so clear in the Tanakh that that is His heart that is His desire, **it is His plan** and all for the express purpose of being able to have a **personal relationship with us!!** You must see this, there is no control here, no strings, and it is our free will. We are drawn to Abba by His **unconditional love, love without expectation!**

In relation to God's Word, we must be very cautious in interpreting His Word. I believe man takes an awful lot of liberty in retelling God what He is really saying. We have evidence of this in the sheer number of denominations that exist today, which are man-made and not God made or ordained by Abba. Denominations are merely offshoots of God's Word in that each denomination has specific tenets that define what they believe based upon their interpretation of His Word. Any non-denominational body of believers that truly follows God's Word and does not **add to or take away** from what God says, are on the right path.

Paul was absolutely distraught over the early churches breaking up into different followings.

4 "I thank my God always for you because of God's love and kindness given to you through the Messiah Yeshua,

5 in that you have been enriched by Him in so many ways, particularly in power of speech and depth of knowledge.

6 Indeed the testimony about the Messiah has become firmly established in you;

7 so that you are not lacking any spiritual gift and are **eagerly awaiting the revealing of our Lord Yeshua the Messiah.**

8 He will enable you to hold out until the end and **thus be blameless on the day of our Lord Yeshua the Messiah-**

9 God is trustworthy: it was He who called you into **fellowship** with His Son, Yeshua the Messiah our Lord.

10 Nevertheless, brothers, I call on you in the name of our Lord Yeshua the Messiah to agree, all of you in what you say, and **not to let yourselves remain split into factions but to be restored to having a common mind and a common purpose.**

11 For some of Chloe's people have made it known to me, my brothers, that there are quarrels among you.

12 I say this because one of you says, 'I follow Sha'ul (Paul)'; another says, 'I follow Apollos'; another, 'I follow 'Kefa (Peter)'; while still another says, 'I follow the Messiah!'

¹³ Has the Messiah been split in pieces? Was it Sha'ul who was put to death on a stake for you? Were you immersed into the name of Sha'ul? ¹⁴ I thank God that I didn't immerse any of you except Crispus and Gaius- ¹⁵ otherwise someone might say that you were indeed immersed into my name" (1 Corinthians 1:4-15).

Paul recognized the enemy's hand in this and knew these divisions had to stop; they would take the focus off of the real truth of Messiah Yeshua's death on the cross and the life the Church is called to live. For the church to believe today, that our divisions are not of the accuser, that he has not infiltrated the church, is naive. The divided Body is the accusers counterfeit to Messiah's **one true Bride**. To believe that your denomination is correct is naïve; that yours is the only **"true"** church is naive. This is one of those times of choosing of man's word over God's word and that is a slippery slope, one you do not want to be on.

Some of the differences in the denominations today are just distractions from the Messiah; they are not heaven or hell differences, just plain and simple distractions from what matters. Some of the differences are much more significant and have quite different consequences: the acceptance of abortion, the acceptance of the practice of homosexuality in the church, anti-Semitism, bigotry, not trusting God's word, the acceptance of sexual sin. You must remember; it is all about God's plan, not our plan. Abba makes it clear in His Word that He is not in favor of **"factions."** Paul could not have stated it better or clearer.

Abba wants sinful man to come to His church, so all should be accepted in; it is for repentance, for their redemption from a sinful state, it is for rebirth, for restoration, being freed from bondage, to become a new creation in Messiah Yeshua!

Father teach us to become one in you, help us to see if we cannot get along here on earth, if we cannot trust you... Heaven is so very far away, but through you we may draw close and learn to be your Bride, without spot or wrinkle!!

Chapter 27

Birthdays

———⚭———

There are two birthday celebrations mentioned in the Bible, Pharaoh's and Herod's.

20 "On the third day, which was Pharaoh's birthday, he gave a party for all his officials, and he lifted up the head of the chief cupbearer and the head of the chief baker among his officials.

21 He restored the chief cupbearer back to his position, so that he again gave Pharaoh his cup.

22 But he hanged the chief baker, as Yosef had interpreted to them" (Genesis 40:20-22).

6 "However, at Herod's birthday celebration, Herodias' daughter danced before the company and pleased Herod so much

⁷ that he promised with an oath to give her whatever she asked.

⁸ Prompted by her mother, she said, 'Give me here on a platter the head of Yochanan the Immerser.'

⁹ The king became deeply upset; but out of regard for the oaths he had sworn before his dinner guests, he ordered that her wish be granted,

¹⁰ and sent and had Yochanan beheaded in prison.

¹¹ The head was brought on a platter to the girl, and she gave it to her mother" (Matthew 14:6-11).

If you look into the origination of birthdays, you will find they are rooted in paganism. They were not celebrated by God's people; we never hear of a birthday celebration in Yeshua's honor, in Moses' or Paul's honor, they did not celebrate birthdays, it just was not done. This is why you never hear of any other birthday celebrations in the bible. This is another celebration we as believers blindly accept without question. When you think about how a birthday is celebrated, it is a day all about the individual, which is rooted in selfishness. It's all about me and what I want.

If it was a pagan celebration in 500 BC, it is a pagan celebration today. Because we say it is not, that does not make it okay. Since we have been celebrating birthdays for 700 years (I made this number up, I do not know when we started celebrating birthdays), that does not make it okay. Since we do not behead or hang people, that does not make it okay. We so often have a blind eye to the accuser and his ways. It is just very subtle angel of light deception. If he can get us to follow **ANYTHING** he has to offer, no matter how trivial, he won that battle, that skirmish. We do not see that some of the things we do today make us the Pharisees or Sadducees of Messiah's day. I do not want to cede him any territory, not one millimeter. The church needs to take back the ground we've lost to the enemy. It is time to trust our Abba, to believe His absolute Word absolutely!!!

Father, Our heart's cry is for our life to be pleasing to You. If anything in our life is not pleasing to you, please show us and teach us how to change it.

Chapter 28

Remove These Chains Father and Restore Your Church, take us back to the Garden

---

Five out of the seven churches are in bondage and must be freed from these chains to move forward in the freedom of the Lord. Only God offers true freedom. **Any** other **"freedom"** outside of His Word, isn't freedom, it is bondage, for anything outside of God's word is bondage and or sin.

As a believer our desire should always be to please God, to want to do His will, to be found pleasing to Him, to be working for Him. When we strike out on our own, in our own thoughts, our own ideas that go against His word, the results will be ours and not His and will be birthed in sin. Abba truly has a perfect plan and when followed will bring the best results, the best fruit. This should always be our desire, to be found pleasing to our God, to follow Him in His Word, in His ways, not ours, not men.

Not all our errors are sinful, but they may not be what's best or what's pleasing to Abba. Living a life pleasing to God is His perfect will. We really cannot believe living a life outside of God's Word would be considered pleasing to Him, that it would be His perfect will, that it would be His perfect plan!!

[11] "'For I know what plans I have in mind for you,' says Adonai, 'plans for wellbeing, not for bad things; so that you can have hope and a future,

[12] When you call to Me and pray to Me, I will listen to you.

*[13] **When you seek me, you will find me, provided you seek me wholeheartedly**;*

[14] and I will let you find Me,' says Adonai. 'Then I will reverse your exile. I will gather you from the nations and places where I have driven you,' says Adonai, 'and bring you back to the place from which I exiled you'" (Jeremiah 29:11-14).

Yahweh tells us in His word that it His desire that **"ALL"** men be saved.

*4 "He wants **all humanity** to be delivered and come to full knowledge of the truth.*

5 For God is one, and there is but one Mediator between God and humanity, Yeshua the Messiah, Himself human,

6 who gave Himself as a ransom on behalf of all, thus providing testimony to God's purpose at just the right time." (1Timothy 2:4-6).

16 "For God so loved the world that He gave His only and unique Son, so that everyone who trusts in Him may have eternal life, instead of being utterly destroyed.

*17 For God did not send the Son into the world to judge the world, but rather so that through Him, **the world** might be saved"* (John 3:16-17).

He goes on to tell us that we are the salt for the land that we are the light of the world, and we are to spread the Gospel to all nations, to a lost and dying world.

¹³ *"You are salt for the land. But if salt becomes tasteless, how can it be made salty again? It is no longer good for anything except being thrown out for people to trample on.*
¹⁴ *You are light for the world. A town built on a hill cannot be hidden.*
¹⁵ *Like-wise, when people light a lamp, they don't cover it with a bowl, but put it on a lampstand, so that it shines for everyone in the house.*
¹⁶ *In the same way, let your light shine before people, so that they may see the good things you do and praise your Father in heaven"* (Matthew 5:13-16).
¹⁵ *"Then He said to them, 'As you go throughout the world, proclaim the Good News to all creation.*
¹⁶ *Whoever trusts and is immersed will be saved; whoever does not trust will be condemned'"* (Mark 16:15-16).

God's plan was that Eretz Yisra'el and His people be the physical manifestation of His love. People would see His love by their very presence in the land that He gave them and by the stories of how they got there. The Church today was supposed to be the physical manifestation of His presence and love. We have abandoned our call and responsibilities given us by our God. The Good News is no longer shared, but often kept within the four walls of the building.

It is time we return to the God of Abraham, Isaac and Jacob, to repent and do the works of God; To trust in the one who was sent, our Messiah. Trusting Him will produce His results, His will, and His plan for a lost and dying world. When we are living a life not pleasing to Abba, we are in exile. But His promise is that He will reverse our exile and bring us back "to the place from which I exiled you provided you seek me wholeheartedly."

Abba, our story is done and our hearts are yours, our lives are yours, our breath is yours. Abba, it is our deep desire to do your will, to walk your path, to follow you in all your ways. We pray for your guidance in all we do. It is through our trust in You that we are able to stand in You! Abba, your Bride desires to "Rise Up" and to reflect who You truly are to this hurt and dying world. Abba, we desire Your Heart Father, Your Mind, and Your Perspective. So, we ask, Abba, that You "Break Every Chain" that binds us and prevents us from walking in YOU. In the name of the true Lord Jesus our Paschal Lamb, through and by His Blood, we speak healing over your Bride, that all chains would break and your true worshippers would be free and stand boldly in You!!

In the Holy and Mighty name of Messiah Yeshua, Amen and Amen

CPSIA information can be obtained
at www.ICGtesting.com
Printed in the USA
FFOW03n1907100217
32258FF